Holt California Mathematics

Course 2
Know-It Notebook™

HOLT, RINEHART AND WINSTON

A Harcourt Education Company

Orlando • **Austin** • New York • San Diego • London

ISBN-13: 978-0-03-094579-3
ISBN-10: 0-03-094579-8

12 11 10 9 8 7   073 14 13 12 11 10 09

Contents

Holt Mathematics

Holt Mathematics

USING THE *KNOW-IT NOTEBOOK*™

This *Know-It Notebook* will help you take notes, organize your thinking, and study for quizzes and tests. There are *Know-It Notes™* pages for every lesson in your textbook. These notes will help you identify important mathematical information that you will need later.

Know-It Notes

Lesson Objectives
A good note-taking practice is to know the objective the content covers.

Vocabulary
Another good note-taking practice is to keep a list of the new vocabulary.
- Use the page references or the glossary in your textbook to find each definition.
- Write each definition on the lines provided.

Additional Examples
Your textbook includes examples for each math concept taught. Additional examples in the *Know-It Notebook* help you take notes so you remember how to solve different types of problems.
- Take notes as your teacher discusses each example.
- Write notes in the blank boxes to help you remember key concepts.
- Write final answers in the shaded boxes.

Check It Out!
Complete the Check It Out! problems that follow some lessons. Use these to make sure you understand the math concepts covered in the lesson.
- Write each answer in the space provided.
- Check your answers with your teacher or another student.
- Ask your teacher to help you understand any problem that you answered incorrectly.

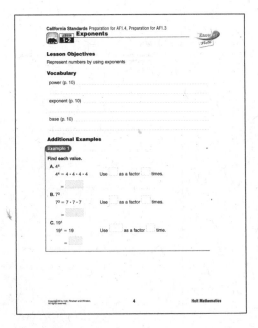

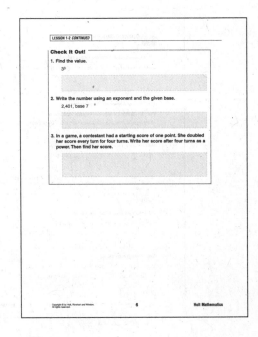

Holt Mathematics

Chapter Review

Complete Chapter Review problems that follow each chapter. This is a good review before you take the chapter test.

- Write each answer in the space provided.
- Check your answers with your teacher or another student.
- Ask your teacher to help you understand any problem that you answered incorrectly.

Big Ideas

The Big Ideas have you summarize the important chapter concepts in your own words. You must think about and understand ideas to put them in your own words. This will also help you remember them.

- Write each answer in the space provided.
- Check your answers with your teacher or another student.
- Ask your teacher to help you understand any question that you answered incorrectly.

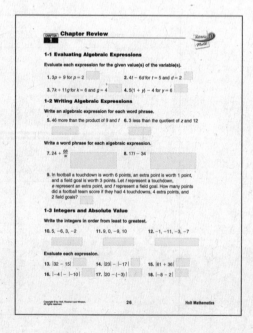

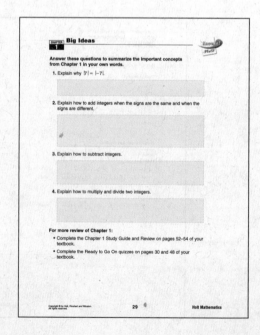

Holt Mathematics

NOTE TAKING STRATEGIES

Taking good notes is very important in many of your classes and will be even more important when you take college classes. This notebook was designed to help you get started. Here are some other steps that can help you take good notes.

Getting Ready

1. Use a loose-leaf notebook. You can add pages to this where and when you want to. It will help keep you organized.

During the Lecture

2. If you are taking notes during a lecture, write the big ideas. Use abbreviations to save time. Do not worry about spelling or writing every word. Use headings to show changes in the topics discussed. Use numbering or bullets to organize supporting ideas under each topic heading. Leave space before each new heading so that you can fill in more information later.

After the Lecture

3. As soon as possible after the lecture, read through your notes and add any information that will help you understand them when you review later. You should also summarize the information into key words or key phrases. This will help your comprehension and will help you process the information. These key words and key phrases will be your memory cues when you are reviewing for or taking a test. At this time you may also want to write questions to help clarify the meaning of the ideas and facts.

4. Read your notes out loud. As you do this, state the ideas in your own words and do as much as you can by memory. This will help you remember and will also help with your thinking process. This activity will help you understand the information.

5. Reflect upon the information you have learned. Ask yourself how new information relates to information you already know. Ask how this relates to your personal experience. Ask how you can apply this information and why it is important.

Before the Test

6. Review your notes. Don't wait until the night before the test to review. Do frequent reviews. Don't just read through your notes. Put the information in your notes into your own words. If you do this you will be able to connect the new material with material you already know, and you will be better prepared for tests. You will have less test anxiety and better recall.

7. Summarize your notes. This should be in your own words and should only include the main points you need to remember. This will help you internalize the information.

Holt Mathematics

LESSON 1-1

Evaluating Algebraic Expressions

Lesson Objectives

Evaluate algebraic expressions

Vocabulary

expression (p. 6) _____

_____

variable (p. 6) _____

_____

numerical expression (p. 6) _____

_____

evaluate (p. 6) _____

_____

Additional Examples

Example 1

Evaluate each expression for the given value of the variable.

A. $x - 5$ for $x = 12$

 $- 5$ Substitute [12] for x.

    Subtract.

B. $2y + 1$ for $y = 4$

$2($ [4] $) + 1$ Substitute [4] for y.

 $+ 1$ Multiply.

    Add.

1

Holt Mathematics

Evaluate each expression for the given value of the variable.

C. $6(n + 2) - 4$ for $n = 5, 6, 7$

n	Substitute	Parentheses	Multiply	Subtract
5	6(___ + 2) − 4	6(___) − 4	___ − 4	
6	6(___ + 2) − 4	6(___) − 4	___ − 4	
7	6(___ + 2) − 4	6(___) − 4	___ − 4	

Example 2

Evaluate each expression for the given values of the variables.

A. $4x + 3y$ for $x = 2$ and $y = 1$

$4($ ___ $) + 3($ ___ $)$ Substitute ___ for x and ___ for y.

___ $+$ ___ Multiply.

___ Add.

B. $9r - 2p$ for $r = 3$ and $p = 5$

$9($ ___ $) - 2($ ___ $)$ Substitute ___ for r and ___ for p.

___ $-$ ___ Multiply.

___ Subtract.

Example 3

Use the expression $1.8c + 32$ to convert each boiling point temperature from degrees Celsius to degrees Fahrenheit.

A. Boiling point of water at sea level: 100°C

$1.8($ ___ $) + 32$ Substitute ___ for c.

___ $+ 32$ Multiply.

___ Add. At sea level, water boils at ___ °F.

Holt Mathematics

Use the expression 1.8c + 32 to convert each boiling point temperature from degrees Celsius to degrees Fahrenheit.

B. Boiling point of water at an altitude of 4400 meters: 85°C

1.8( ) + 32   Substitute [ ] for c.

[ ] + 32   Multiply.

[ ]   Add.

At an altitude of 4400 meters, water boils at [ ] °F.

Check It Out!

1. Evaluate the expression for the given value of the variable.

4c + 1 for c = 11

2. Evaluate the expression for the given value of the variables.

8q − 3r for q = 2 and r = 2

3. Use the expression 1.8c + 32 to convert the boiling point temperature from degrees Celsius to degrees Fahrenheit.

10°C

Holt Mathematics

Writing Algebraic Expressions

LESSON 1-2

Lesson Objectives

Translate between algebraic expressions and word phrases

Additional Examples

Example 1

Write an algebraic expression for each word phrase.

A. 9 less than a number w

w decreased by 9

w [—] 9

[   ]

B. 3 increased by the difference of p and 5

the difference of p and 5

p [—] 5

3 increased by the difference of p and 5

$3 + (p - 5)$

Example 2

Write a word phrase for the algebraic expression $9 - 3c$.

$9 - 3$ [   ] c

9 [   ] the [   ] of 3 and c

[   ]

Holt Mathematics

Example 3

A restaurant leased its banquet hall for a function. The cost was $10 per person. Write an algebraic expression to evaluate what the cost would be if 20, 21, 22, or 23 people attended the function.

$10   per   person   [   ]

Combine *n* equal amounts of $10. Evaluate for *n* = 20, 21, 22, and 23.

n	Substitute	Multiply
20	$10 · ([ ])	
21	$10 · ([ ])	
22	$10 · ([ ])	
23	$10 · ([ ])	

Example 4

Write a word problem that can be evaluated by the algebraic expression 27 + *t*. Then evaluate the expression for *t* = 1.76.

27 + *t*   Write the expression.

27 + [   ]   Substitute [   ] for *t*.

[   ]   Add.

The total cost of the sweater was [   ].

Holt Mathematics

Check It Out!

1. Write an algebraic expression for the word phrase.

   The quotient of a number f and 6

2. Write a word phrase for the algebraic expression $17 + 19b$.

3. Gasoline costs $1.99 per n gallons. What will the cost be for 10, 12, 14, and 15 gallons?

4. Write a word problem that can be evaluated by the algebraic expression $43 - d$, and evaluate the expression for $d = 10.24$.

Holt Mathematics

Integers and Absolute Value

LESSON
1-3

Lesson Objectives

Compare and order integers and simplify expressions containing absolute values

Vocabulary

integers (p. 14) _____

_____

opposite (p. 14) _____

_____

absolute value (p. 15) _____

_____

Additional Examples

Example 1

After one round of golf, the scores are Aaron 4 and Felicity −1.

A. Use <, >, or = to compare the scores. Aaron's score is 4, and Felicity's score is −1.

$$\overset{\longleftarrow\;\longrightarrow}{\underset{-3\;-2\;-1\;\;0\;\;1\;\;2\;\;3\;\;4\;\;5}{\;}}$$

Place the scores on a number line.

[   ]

−1 is to the [   ] of 4.

B. List the golfers' scores in order from the lowest to the highest. The scores are −4, 2, 5, and −3.

$$\overset{\longleftarrow\;\longrightarrow}{\underset{-5\;-4\;-3\;-2\;-1\;\;0\;\;1\;\;2\;\;3\;\;4\;\;5}{\;}}$$

Place the scores on a number line and read them from left to right.

In order from the lowest to the highest, the scores are

[   ].

Holt Mathematics

Example 2

Write the integers 8, −5, and 4 in order from least to greatest.

Graph the integers on a number line. Then read them from left to right.

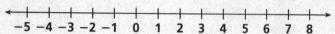

The integers in order from least to greatest are ⬚ .

Example 3

Simplify each expression.

A. $|-3|$

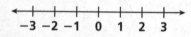   −3 is ⬚ units from 0, so $|-3| =$ ⬚ .

B. $|17-6|$

$|17-6| = |11|$ Subtract first.

$= 11$ Then find the absolute value: 11 is ⬚ units from 0.

C. $|-8| + |-5|$ Find the absolute values first.

$|-8| =$ ⬚   −8 is ⬚ units from 0.

$|-5| =$ ⬚   −5 is ⬚ units from 0.

$8 + 5 = 13$ Then add.

D. $|5 + 1| + |8 - 6|$

$|5 + 1| + |8 - 6| = |6| + |2|$ $5 + 1 = 6$; $8 - 6 = 2$

$= 6 + 2$ 6 is ⬚ from 0; 2 is ⬚ from 0.

$= 8$

Holt Mathematics

Check It Out!

1. List the golfers' scores in order from the lowest to the highest. The scores are −3, 1, 0, and −2.

2. Write the integers −4, −5, and 4 in order from least to greatest.

3. Simplify the expression |12 − 4|.

Holt Mathematics

California Standards ← NS1.2, ← AF1.3

Adding Integers

LESSON 1-4

Know it!
Note

Lesson Objectives

Add integers

additive inverse (p. 18) _____

_____

Additional Examples

Example 1

Use a number line to find each sum.

A. $(-6) + 2$

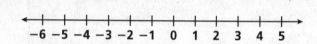

−6 −5 −4 −3 −2 −1 0 1 2 3 4 5

You finish at ⬚, so $(-6) + 2 =$ ▢ .

Start at 0.

Move ⬚ 6 units.

From ⬚, move ⬚ 2 units.

B. $-3 + (-6)$

−9 −8 −7 −6 −5 −4 −3 −2 −1 0 1

You finish at ⬚, so $-3 + (-6) =$ ▢ .

Start at 0.

Move left ⬚ units.

From ⬚, move left ⬚ units.

Example 2

Add.

A. $1 + (-2)$

▢

Think: Find the ⬚ of 2 and 1.

$2 > 1$; use the sign of ⬚ .

B. $(-8) + 5$

▢

Think: Find the ⬚ of 8 and 5.

$8 > 5$; use the sign of ⬚ .

Holt Mathematics

Example 3

Evaluate $c + 4$ for $c = -8$.

$c + 4$

$(\boxed{}) + 4$ Replace c with $\boxed{}$.

Think: Find the $\boxed{}$ of 8 and 4.

$\boxed{} + 4 = \boxed{}$ $8 > 4$; use the sign of $\boxed{}$.

Example 4

Meka opened a new bank account. Find her account balance after the first four transactions, listed below.

Deposits: $200, $20   Withdrawals: $166, $38

$200 + 20 + (-166) + (-38)$ Use a $\boxed{}$ sign for deposits

and a $\boxed{}$ sign for withdrawals.

$(200 + 20) + (-166 + -38)$ Group integers with $\boxed{}$ signs.

$220 + (-204)$ Add integers within each group.

$\boxed{}$ $220 > 204$; use the sign of $\boxed{}$.

Meka's account balance after the first four transactions is $\boxed{}$.

Check It Out!

1. Use a number line to find the sum.

$(-3) + 7$

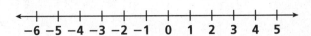

Holt Mathematics

2. Add $(-4) + 1$.

3. Evaluate $d + 7$ for $d = -3$.

4. Michael opened a new bank account. Find his account balance after the first four transactions listed below.

Deposits: $175, $95   Withdrawls: $133, $65

Holt Mathematics

California Standards ◆━NS1.2, ◆━NS2.5

LESSON 1-5

Subtracting Integers

Lesson Objectives

Subtract integers

Additional Examples

Example 1

Subtract.

A. $-7 - 4$

$-7 - 4 = -7 + ($ ⬚ $)$ Add the ⬚ of 4.

= ⬚   Same sign; use the sign of the integers.

B. $8 - (-5)$

$8 - (-5) = 8$ ⬚ 5 Add the ⬚ of -5.

= ⬚   Same sign; use the sign of the ⬚.

C. $-6 - (-3)$

$-6 - (-3) = -6$ ⬚ 3 Add the opposite of ⬚.

= ⬚ $6 > 3$; use the sign of ⬚.

Example 2

Evaluate each expression for the given value of the variable.

A. $-9 - y$ for $y = -4$

$-9 - y$

$-9 - ($ ⬚ $)$ Substitute -4 for ⬚.

$= -9$ ⬚ 4 Add the opposite of ⬚.

= ⬚ $9 > 4$; use the ⬚ of 9.

Holt Mathematics

Evaluate each expression for the given value of the variable.

B. $n - 6$ for $n = -2$

$n - 6$

$\boxed{} - 6$ Substitute -2 for $\boxed{}$.

$-2 - 6$ Same sign; use the sign of the $\boxed{}$.

$\boxed{}$

C. $|8 - j| + |-2|$ for $j = -6$

$|8 - j| + |-2|$

$|8 - (\boxed{})| + |-2|$ Substitute $\boxed{}$ for j.

$= |8 \boxed{} 6| + |-2|$ Add the $\boxed{}$ of -6.

$= |\boxed{}| + |-2|$ The absolute value of 14 is $\boxed{}$, and the

                absolute value of -2 is $\boxed{}$.

$= 14 + \boxed{}$

$= 16$ Add.

Example 3

The top of the Sears Tower, in Chicago, is 1454 feet above street level, while the lowest level is 43 feet below street level. How far is it from the lowest level to the top?

$1454 - (-43)$ Subtract the distance below street level from the distance above street level.

$= 1454 + \boxed{}$ Add the opposite of -43.

$= \boxed{}$ Same sign; use the sign of the integers.

It is $\boxed{}$ feet from bottom to top.

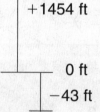

+1454 ft

0 ft

−43 ft

Holt Mathematics

Check It Out!

1. Subtract.

$$-7 - (-8)$$

2. Evaluate the expression for the given value of the variable.

$-5 - r$ for $r = -2$

3. The distance from the high dive to the swimming pool is 10 feet. The pool is 12 feet deep. What is the total distance from the high dive to the bottom of the pool?

Holt Mathematics

LESSON 1-6

Multiplying and Dividing Integers

Lesson Objectives

Multiply and divide integers

Additional Examples

 Example 1

Multiply or divide.

A. $-6(4)$ Signs are ☐

☐   Answer is ☐ .

B. $-8(-5)(2)$ Multiply ☐ of the integers. Signs are the ☐

☐   Answer is ☐ .

C. $\dfrac{-18}{2}$ ☐ are different.

☐   Answer is ☐ .

D. $\dfrac{-25}{-5}$ ☐ are the same.

☐   Answer is ☐ .

Example 2

Simplify.

A. $3(-6-12)$ Subtract inside the ☐ .

$= 3($ ☐ $)$ Think: The signs are ☐ .

$=$ ☐   The answer is ☐ .

B. $-5(-5+2)$ Add inside the ☐ .

$= -5($ ☐ $)$ Think: The ☐ are the same.

$=$ ☐   The answer is ☐ .

Holt Mathematics

Example 3

A golfer plays 5 holes. On 3 holes, he is 4 strokes over par. On 2 holes, he is 4 strokes under par. Each score over par can be represented by a positive integer, and each score under par can be represented by a negative integer. Find the total score relative to par.

$3(4) + 2(-4)$ Add the losses to the gains.

= ☐ + (☐)   Multiply.

= ☐   Add.   The golfer was ☐ strokes over par.

Check It Out!

1. Multiply or divide.

$-3(-2)(4)$

2. Simplify.

$-3(6) - 9$

3. A golfer plays 7 holes. On 3 holes, he is 3 strokes over par. On 4 holes he is 3 strokes under par. Each score over par can be represented by a positive integer, and each score under par can be represented by a negative integer. Find the total score relative to par.

Holt Mathematics

LESSON 1-7
Solving Equations by Adding or Subtracting

Lesson Objectives

Solve equations using addition and subtraction

Vocabulary

equation (p. 32) _____

_____

inverse operations (p. 32) _____

Additional Examples

Example 1

Determine which value of x is a solution of the equation.

$x + 8 = 15$; $x = 5, 7,$ or 23

Substitute each value for x in the equation.

$x + 8 = 15$

$5 + \boxed{} \overset{?}{=} 15$ Substitute $\boxed{}$ for x.

$\boxed{} \overset{?}{=} 15$ ✗   So 5 ░░░░░ a solution.

$x + 8 = 15$

$\boxed{} + 8 \overset{?}{=} 15$ ░░░░░ 7 for x.

$\boxed{} \overset{?}{=} 15$ ✓   So 7 ░░░░░ a solution.

$x + 8 = 15$

$\boxed{} + 8 \overset{?}{=} 15$ Substitute 23 for $\boxed{}$.

$\boxed{} \overset{?}{=} 15$ ✗   So 23 ░░░░░ a solution.

Example 2

Solve.

$$10 + n = 18$$

$$\underline{} - \boxed{} \qquad - \boxed{}$$

$$\boxed{} + n = \boxed{}$$

Since $\boxed{}$ is added to n, subtract $\boxed{}$ from both sides to undo the addition.

$$n = \boxed{}$$

Identity $\boxed{}$ of Zero:

$$0 + n = n$$

Example 3

Net force is the sum of all forces acting on an object. Expressed in newtons (N), it tells you in which direction and how quickly the object will move. Jan and Alex are arguing over who gets to play a board game. If Jan, on the right, pulls with a force of 14 N, what force is Alex exerting on the game if the net force is 3 N?

1. Understand the Problem

The **answer** is the force that $\boxed{}$ is exerting on the game.

List the important information:

- Jan, on the right, pulls with a force of $\boxed{}$.

- The net force is $\boxed{}$.

Show the relationship of the information:

$$\boxed{} = \text{Jan's force} + \text{Alex's force}$$

2. Make a Plan

Write an equation and solve it. Let f represent $\boxed{}$ force on the game, and use the equation model.

$$\boxed{}$$

Holt Mathematics

3. **Solve**

$$3 = f + 14$$
$$\underline{-14} \qquad \underline{-14}$$ Subtract ⬜ from both sides.

$$\boxed{} = f$$

Alex is exerting a force of ⬜ newtons on the game.

4. **Look Back**

Alex exerts force to the left, so the force is ⬜. Its

absolute value is ⬜ than the force Jan exerts on the right. This

makes sense, since the net force is ⬜; thus the game is

being pulled closer to ⬜.

Check It Out!

1. Determine which value of *x* is a solution of the equation.

$$x - 4 = 13; x = 9, 17, \text{ or } 27$$

2. Solve.

$$44 = y - 23$$

3. Frankie and Carol are playing tug of war using a rope. If Frankie, on the right, pulls with a force of 7 N, what force is Carol exerting on the game if the net force is 4 N?

Holt Mathematics

LESSON 1-8 Solving Equations by Multiplying or Dividing

Lesson Objectives

Solve equations using multiplication and division

Vocabulary

Identity Property of Multiplication (p. 37) _____

_____

Division Property of Multiplication (p. 37) _____

_____

_____

Additional Examples

Example 1

Solve.

$-9y = 45$

$\boxed{}\,y = 45$

$\dfrac{\boxed{}}{} \quad \dfrac{\boxed{}}{}$

$\boxed{}\,y = \boxed{}$

$y = \boxed{}$

Since y is $\boxed{}$ -9, divide both sides

by $\boxed{}$ to $\boxed{}$ the multiplication.

$\boxed{}$ Property of Multiplication

Example 2

Solve.

$\dfrac{b}{-4} = 5$

$\boxed{} \cdot \dfrac{b}{-4} = \boxed{} \cdot 5$

$1 \cdot b = \boxed{}$

$b = \boxed{}$

Since b is divided by $\boxed{}$, multiply both

sides by $\boxed{}$ to undo the division.

Identity Property of Multiplication: $1 \cdot b = \boxed{}$

Holt Mathematics

Example 3

It takes 450 person-hours to prepare a convention center for a conference. The director of the convention center assigns 25 people to the job. If each person works the same number of hours, how long does each person work?

Let x represent the number of hours each person works.

number of people · number of hours each person works = total number of person-hours

☐ · ☐ = ☐

$25x = 450$ Write the equation.

$\dfrac{25x}{\boxed{}} = \dfrac{450}{\boxed{}}$ Since x is multiplied by ☐, divide both sides by ☐ to undo the multiplication.

$1 \cdot x = \boxed{}$ Identity Property of Multiplication: $1 \cdot x = \boxed{}$

$x = \boxed{}$ Each person works for ☐ hours.

Check It Out!

1. Solve.

   $-3y = 36$

2. Solve.

   $\dfrac{c}{-3} = 5$

3. It takes 320 person-hours to prepare a concert hall for a concert. The director of the concert hall assigns 16 people to the job. If each person works the same number of hours, how long does each person work?

Holt Mathematics

California Standards ◄━ AF4.1, AF1.1

LESSON 1-9

Solving Two-Step Equations

Lesson Objectives

Solve two-step equations

Additional Examples

Example 1

Translate each sentence into an equation.

A. 17 less than the quotient of a number *x* and 2 is 21.

$(x \div \boxed{}) - \boxed{} = 21$

$\boxed{} - \boxed{} = \boxed{}$

B. Twice a number *m* increased by −4 is 0.

$\boxed{} \cdot m + \boxed{} = 0$

$\boxed{} + \boxed{} = \boxed{}$

Example 2

Solve.

A. $3x + 4 = -11$

Step 1: $3x + 4 = -11$ Since 4 is added to 3*x*, subtract $\boxed{}$ from both sides to undo the addition.

$\underline{- \boxed{}} = \underline{- \boxed{}}$

$3x = \boxed{}$

Step 2: 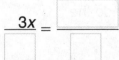 $\dfrac{3x}{\boxed{}} = \dfrac{\boxed{}}{\boxed{}}$ Since *x* is multiplied by 3, divide both sides by

$\boxed{}$ to undo the multiplication.

$x = \boxed{}$

Holt Mathematics

B. $8 = -5y - 2$

Step 1: $\qquad 8 = -5y - 2$

Since 2 is subtracted from $-5y$, add to both sides to undo the subtraction.

$$\dfrac{\boxed{}}{\boxed{}} = \dfrac{\boxed{}}{}$$

$$\boxed{} = -5y$$

Step 2: $\dfrac{\boxed{}}{\boxed{}} = \dfrac{-5y}{\boxed{}}$

Since y is multiplied by -5, divide both sides by $\boxed{}$ to undo the multiplication.

$$\boxed{} = y$$

Example 3

Solve.

A. $4 + \dfrac{m}{7} = 9$

$\qquad 4 + \dfrac{m}{7} = 9$

Since 4 is added to $\dfrac{m}{7}$, subtract $\boxed{}$ from both sides to undo the addition.

$$-\dfrac{\boxed{}}{} = -\dfrac{\boxed{}}{}$$

$$\dfrac{m}{7} = \boxed{}$$

Since m is divided by 7, multiply both sides by $\boxed{}$ to undo the division.

$$7 \cdot \dfrac{m}{7} = \boxed{} \cdot \boxed{}$$

$$m = \boxed{}$$

B. $14 = \dfrac{z}{2} - 3$

Since 3 is $\boxed{}$ $\dfrac{z}{2}$,

$\qquad 14 = \dfrac{z}{2} - 3$

add $\boxed{}$ to both sides to undo the $\boxed{}$.

$$\dfrac{\boxed{}}{\boxed{}} = \dfrac{\boxed{}}{}$$

$$\boxed{} = \dfrac{z}{2}$$

Since z is divided by $\boxed{}$, multiply both sides

$$\boxed{} \cdot 17 = \boxed{} \cdot \dfrac{z}{2}$$

by $\boxed{}$ to undo the $\boxed{}$.

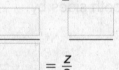

$$\boxed{} = z$$

Holt Mathematics

Example 4

Donna buys a DVD player that costs $120, and several DVDs that cost $14 each. She spends a total of $204. How many DVDs does she buy?

Let d represent the number of DVDs that Donna buys.

cost of DVD player + cost of DVDs = total cost

$120 + \qquad $14 \cdot d = \qquad $204

$120 + 14d = 204$ \qquad Since 120 is added to $14d$, subtract ☐ from both sides to undo the addition.

$-$☐ $= -$☐

$14d =$ ☐

$\dfrac{14d}{☐} = \dfrac{☐}{☐}$ \qquad Since d is multiplied by 14, divide both sides by ☐ to undo the multiplication.

$d =$ ☐ \qquad Donna buys ☐ DVDs.

Check It Out!

1. Translate the sentence into an equation.

Three less than the quotient of a number x and 4 is 7.

2. Solve.

$7x + 1 = -13$

3. Solve.

$2 + \dfrac{k}{6} = 9$

4. John buys an MP3 player that costs $249, and several songs that cost $0.99 each. He spends a total of $278. How many songs does he buy?

Holt Mathematics

Chapter Review

1-1 Evaluating Algebraic Expressions

Evaluate each expression for the given value(s) of the variable(s).

1. $3p + 9$ for $p = 2$

2. $4t - 6d$ for $t = 5$ and $d = 2$

3. $7k + 11g$ for $k = 6$ and $g = 4$

4. $5(1 + y) - 4$ for $y = 6$

1-2 Writing Algebraic Expressions

Write an algebraic expression for each word phrase.

5. 46 more than the product of 9 and f

6. 3 less than the quotient of z and 12

Write a word phrase for each algebraic expression.

7. $24 + \dfrac{68}{w}$

8. $17l - 34$

9. In football a touchdown is worth 6 points, an extra point is worth 1 point, and a field goal is worth 3 points. Let t represent a touchdown, e represent an extra point, and f represent a field goal. How many points did a football team score if they had 4 touchdowns, 4 extra points, and 2 field goals?

1-3 Integers and Absolute Value

Write the integers in order from least to greatest.

10. $5, -6, 3, -2$

11. $9, 0, -9, 10$

12. $-1, -11, -3, -7$

Evaluate each expression.

13. $|32 - 15|$

14. $|23| - |-17|$

15. $|61 + 36|$

16. $|-4| - |-10|$

17. $|20 - (-3)|$

18. $|-8 - 2|$

1-4 Adding Integers

Add.

19. $-21 + 12$

20. $-13 + 19$

21. $11 + (-4)$

Evaluate each expression for the given value of the variable.

22. $12 + t$ for $t = -8$

23. $u + 9$ for $u = -3$

24 $j + (-6)$ for $j = 17$

25. Timothy scored 114 points during his first basketball season. The second basketball season he scored 307 points. How many more points did Timothy score in his second season than his first season?

1-5 Subtracting Integers

Subtract.

26. $-9 - (-6)$

27. $-17 - 2$

28. $3 - (-11)$

Evaluate each expression for the given value of the variable.

29. $20 - r$ for $r = -1$

30. $-32 - x$ for $x = 17$

31. $-23 - q$ for $q = -9$

32. On a Wednesday in early March, the temperature rose from $-2°F$ to $57°F$. By how many degrees Fahrenheit did the temperature change?

1-6 Multiplying and Dividing Integers

Multiply or divide.

33. $(7)(-5)$

34. $\dfrac{36}{-9}$

35. $(-7)(2)(-1)$

Simplify.

36. $2(-6 - 2)$

37. $4(3 - 7)$

38. $(-3)(11 - 2)$

39. An elevator descends 2 feet every second. Write an integer to represent the height of the elevator. Find an integer to represent the change in the elevator's height after 1.25 minutes.

Holt Mathematics

1-7 Solving Equations by Adding or Subtracting

Solve.

40. $t + 21 = 37$ **41.** $45 - h = 28$ **42.** $g - (-9) = 15$

43. A group of deep-sea divers ascended 574 feet before their final stop to equalize. They stopped 27 feet below the surface. At what depth did they begin their ascent?

1-8 Solving Equations by Multiplying or Dividing

Solve and check.

44. $-7 = \frac{d}{5}$ **45.** $-4c = -28$ **46.** $15 = \frac{90}{v}$

47. Betsy collected 132 dolls. Betsy has 3 times as many dolls as Alicia. How many dolls does Alicia's have?

48. Marcus scored 6 points in his last game. This is $\frac{1}{4}$ the number of points he usually scores. How many points does Marcus usually score?

1-9 Solving Two-Step Equations

Solve. Check each answer.

56. $3x + 9 = 72$ **57.** $2q - 7 = 13$ **58.** $-4y + 11 = 75$

59. $38 = 7p - 18$ **60.** $\frac{z}{5} + 1 = 8$ **61.** $\frac{x}{-3} - 9 = 10$

62. A salesperson earned a paycheck for $2,750. The paycheck was a $500 bonus plus a flat rate for three seminars attended. What was the salesperson's rate of pay for each seminar?

Holt Mathematics

Answer these questions to summarize the important concepts from Chapter 1 in your own words.

1. Explain why $|7| = |-7|$.

2. Explain how to add integers when the signs are the same and when the signs are different.

3. Explain how to subtract integers.

4. Explain how to multiply and divide two integers.

For more review of Chapter 1:

- Complete the Chapter 1 Study Guide and Review on pages 52–54 of your textbook.

- Complete the Ready to Go On quizzes on pages 30 and 48 of your textbook.

Holt Mathematics

 **California Standards** ← NS1.5, NS1.3

Rational Numbers

LESSON 2-1

Lesson Objectives

Write rational numbers in equivalent forms

Additional Examples

Example 1

Write each fraction as a decimal.

A. $\frac{11}{9}$

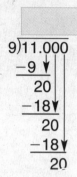

```
9)11.000
 -9 ↓
   20
  -18 ↓
    20
   -18 ↓
     20
```

This is a [____] decimal.

The pattern repeats.

$\frac{11}{9}$ is equivalent to [____]

B. $\frac{7}{20}$

```
20)7.00
  -60
   100
  -100
     0
```

The remainder is zero.

This is a [____] decimal.

$\frac{7}{20}$ is equivalent to [____]

Example 2

Write each decimal as a fraction in simplest form.

0.622

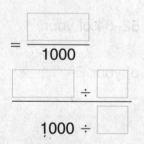

$= \frac{\quad}{1000}$

$= \frac{\quad \div \quad}{1000 \div \quad}$

$= [\quad]$

2 is in the [____] place, so write thousandths as the denominator.

Simplify by [____] by the greatest common divisor.

Holt Mathematics

Example 3

Write 0.$\overline{4}$ as a fraction in simplest form.

$x = 0.444\ldots$ — Let x represent the number.

$\boxed{}x = \boxed{}(0.444\ldots)$ — Multiply both sides by $\boxed{}$ because 1 digit repeats.

$10x = 4.444\ldots$ — Subtract x from both sides to eliminate the repeating part.

$-\boxed{} = \boxed{}$

$9x = 4$ — Since $x = 0.444\ldots$, use $\boxed{}$ for x on the right side of the equation.

$\dfrac{9x}{\boxed{}} = \dfrac{4}{\boxed{}}$ — Since x is multiplied by 9, divide both sides by $\boxed{}$.

$x = \boxed{}$ — Write in simplest form.

0.$\overline{4}$ is equivalent to $\boxed{}$.

Check It Out!

1. Write the fraction as a decimal.

$\dfrac{9}{40}$

2. Write the decimal as a fraction in simplest form.

8.75

3. Write 0.$\overline{36}$ as a fraction in simplest form.

Holt Mathematics

LESSON 2-2 Comparing and Ordering Rational Numbers

Lesson Objectives

Compare and order positive and negative rational numbers written as fractions, decimals, and integers

Vocabulary

least common denominator (LCD) (p. 70) _____

_____

Additional Examples

Example 1

Compare. Write <, >, or =.

A. $\dfrac{5}{6}$ ▇ $\dfrac{7}{10}$

Method 1 Multiply denominators to find a common denominator.

$6 \cdot 10 = \boxed{}$ Multiply $\boxed{}$ and $\boxed{}$ to find a common denominator.

$\dfrac{5}{6} \cdot \dfrac{\boxed{}}{\boxed{}} = \dfrac{5 \cdot 10}{6 \cdot 10} = \dfrac{\boxed{}}{\boxed{}}$ Write the fractions with a common denominator.

$\dfrac{7}{10} \cdot \dfrac{\boxed{}}{\boxed{}} = \dfrac{7 \cdot 6}{10 \cdot 6} = \dfrac{\boxed{}}{\boxed{}}$

$\dfrac{50}{60} \boxed{} \dfrac{42}{60}$, so $\dfrac{5}{6} \boxed{} \dfrac{7}{10}$ Compare the fractions.

Holt Mathematics

B. $\dfrac{2}{3}$ ▢ $\dfrac{4}{5}$

Method 2 Find the least common denominator.

3: 3, 6, 9, 12, 15, . . . 5: 5, 10, 15, . . . List multiples of 3 and 5. The LCM

is ▢ .

$\dfrac{2}{3} \cdot \dfrac{\Box}{\Box} = \dfrac{2 \cdot 5}{3 \cdot 5} = \dfrac{\Box}{\Box}$ Write the fractions with a common denominator.

$\dfrac{4}{5} \cdot \dfrac{\Box}{\Box} = \dfrac{4 \cdot 3}{5 \cdot 3} = \dfrac{\Box}{\Box}$

$\dfrac{10}{15}$ ▢ $\dfrac{12}{15}$, so $\dfrac{2}{3}$ ▢ $\dfrac{4}{5}$ Compare the fractions.

Example 2

Compare. Write <, >, or =.

A. $5\dfrac{2}{9}$ ▢ $5\dfrac{2}{7}$

$5\dfrac{2}{9} = $ ▢ and $5\dfrac{2}{7} = $ ▢   Write the fractions as

▢ .

$5.\overline{2}$ ▢ 5.286, so $5\dfrac{2}{9}$ ▢ $5\dfrac{2}{7}$ Compare the decimals.

B. -0.44 ▢ $-\dfrac{2}{5}$

$-\dfrac{2}{5} = $ ▢   Write ▢ as a ▢ .

-0.44 ▢ -0.4, so -0.44 ▢ $-\dfrac{2}{5}$ Compare the decimals.

Holt Mathematics

Example 3

The numbers $\frac{14}{4}$, -3.4, 6.0, and -2.5 represent the percentage of change in populations for four states. List these numbers in order from least to greatest.

Place the numbers on a number line and read them from left to right.

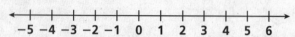

The percent changes in population from least to greatest are -3.4, -2.5, $\frac{14}{4}$, and 6.0.

Check It Out!

1. Compare. Write $<$, $>$, or $=$.

$\frac{2}{3}$ ☐ $\frac{4}{5}$

2. Compare. Write $<$, $>$, or $=$.

-0.80 ☐ $-\frac{4}{5}$

3. The numbers $\frac{7}{2}$, 3.0, -2.2, and -3.9 represent the percent of change in population for four states. List these numbers in order from least to greatest.

Holt Mathematics

LESSON 2-3 Adding and Subtracting Rational Numbers

Know it!
·Note

Lesson Objectives

Add and subtract decimals and rational numbers with like denominators

Additional Examples

Example 1

Add or subtract.

A. $0.3 + (-1.2)$

$$
\begin{array}{r}
0.3 \\
+ (-1.2) \\
\hline
\boxed{}
\end{array}
$$

Line up the decimal points.

Add.

B. $17.2 - 4.39$

$$
\begin{array}{r}
17.20 \\
- 4.39 \\
\hline
\boxed{}
\end{array}
$$

Line up the decimal points. Use zero as a placeholder.

Subtract.

Example 2

In August 2001 at the World University Games in Beijing, China, Jimyria Hicks ran the 200-meter dash in 24.08 seconds. Her best time at the U.S. Senior National Meet in June of the same year was 23.35 seconds. How much faster did she run in June?

$$
\begin{array}{r}
24.08 \\
-23.35 \\
\hline
\boxed{}
\end{array}
$$

Line up the decimal points.

She ran ⬚ second faster in June.

Holt Mathematics

Example 3

Add or subtract. Write each answer in simplest form.

A. $-\dfrac{2}{9} - \dfrac{5}{9}$

$-\dfrac{2}{9} - \dfrac{5}{9} = \dfrac{\boxed{}}{9} = \boxed{}$ Subtract numerators. Keep the denominator.

B. $\dfrac{6}{7} + \left(-\dfrac{3}{7}\right)$

$\dfrac{6}{7} + \left(-\dfrac{3}{7}\right) = \dfrac{\boxed{}}{7} = \boxed{}$ Add numerators. Keep the denominator.

Example 4

Evaluate each expression for the given value of the variable.

$12.1 - x$ for $x = -0.1$

$12.1 - (\boxed{})$ Substitute $\boxed{}$ for x.

$\boxed{}$ Think: $12.1 - (-0.1) = 12.1 \boxed{} 0.1$

Check It Out!

1. Subtract.

$12.4 - 3.29$ $\boxed{}$

2. Tom ran the 100-meter dash in 11.5 seconds last year. This year he improved his time by 0.568 seconds. How fast did Tom run the 100-meter dash this year? $\boxed{}$

3. Add.

$\dfrac{5}{9} + \left(-\dfrac{4}{9}\right)$ $\boxed{}$

4. Evaluate the expression for the given value of the variable.

$52.3 - y$ for $y = -7.8$ $\boxed{}$

Holt Mathematics

Multiplying Rational Numbers

LESSON 2-4

Lesson Objectives

Multiply fractions, mixed numbers, and decimals

Additional Examples

Example 1

Multiply. Write each answer in simplest form.

A. $\frac{1}{8}\left(\frac{6}{7}\right)$

$\frac{1}{8}\left(\frac{6}{7}\right) = \frac{1(6)}{8(7)}$ Multiply _____.

                          Multiply _____.

$= \frac{1(6)}{8(7)}$ Look for common _____ : 2.

$= $ [   ]   Simplify.

B. $-\frac{2}{3}\left(4\frac{1}{2}\right)$

$-\frac{2}{3}\left(4\frac{1}{2}\right) = -\frac{2}{3}\left(\frac{9}{2}\right)$ Rewrite $4\frac{1}{2}$ as an improper fraction:

$4\frac{1}{2} = \frac{4(2) + 1}{2} = \frac{9}{2}$.

$= -\frac{2(9)}{3(2)}$ Multiply _____.

                          Multiply _____.

$= -\frac{2(9)}{3(2)}$ Look for common _____ : 2, 3.

$= $ [   ]   Simplify.

Holt Mathematics

Example 2

Joy completes $\frac{1}{20}$ of her painting each day. How much of her painting does she complete in a 7-day week?

$\frac{1}{20}(7) = \frac{1}{20}\left(\frac{7}{1}\right)$ Write the integer as a fraction: $7 = \frac{7}{1}$

$\frac{1(7)}{20(1)} = \boxed{}$ Multiply $\boxed{}$ and $\boxed{}$.

Joy completes $\boxed{}$ of her painting in a 7-day week.

Example 3

Multiply.

A. $2(-0.51)$

$\begin{array}{r} -0.51 \\ \times 2 \\ \hline \boxed{} \end{array}$ $\boxed{}$ decimal places
$\boxed{}$ decimal places
$\boxed{} + \boxed{} = \boxed{}$ decimal places

B. $(-0.4)(-3.75)$

$\begin{array}{r} -0.4 \\ \times -3.75 \\ \hline 20 \\ 28 \\ 12 \\ \hline \boxed{} \end{array}$ $\boxed{}$ decimal places
$\boxed{}$ decimal places

$\boxed{} + \boxed{} = \boxed{}$ decimal places

Holt Mathematics

Check It Out!

1. Multiply. Write the answer in simplest form.

$$\frac{3}{5}\left(\frac{5}{8}\right)$$

2. Mark runs $\frac{1}{7}$ mile each day. What is the total distance Mark runs in a 5-day week?

3. Multiply.

3.1(0.28)

Holt Mathematics

LESSON 2-5

Dividing Rational Numbers

Lesson Objectives

Divide fractions and decimals

Vocabulary

multiplicative inverse (p. 82) _____

_____

reciprocal (p. 82) _____

_____

Additional Examples

Example 1

Divide. Write each answer in simplest form.

A. $\frac{5}{11} \div \frac{1}{2}$

$\frac{5}{11} \div \frac{1}{2} = \frac{5}{11} \cdot \boxed{}$ Multiply by the $\boxed{}$.

$= \frac{5}{11} \cdot \boxed{}$ No common $\boxed{}$

$= \boxed{}$ Simplest form

B. $2\frac{3}{8} \div 2$

$2\frac{3}{8} \div 2 = \boxed{} \div \frac{2}{1}$ Write as an $\boxed{}$ fraction.

$= \frac{19}{8} \boxed{}$ Multiply by the $\boxed{}$.

$= \frac{19 \cdot 1}{8 \cdot 2}$ No common $\boxed{}$.

$= \boxed{} = \boxed{}$ $19 \div 16 = 1 \text{ R } \boxed{}$

Holt Mathematics

Example 2

Find. 0.384 ÷ 0.24.

$$0.384 \div 0.24 = \frac{0.384}{0.24}\left(\frac{100}{100}\right) = \boxed{}$$

0.24 has 2 decimal places, so multiply both numbers by 100 to make the divisor an integer.
Then divide as with whole numbers.

$$= \boxed{}$$

Example 3

Evaluate.

$\frac{5.25}{n}$ for $n = 0.15$ Substitute 0.15 for n.

$$\frac{5.25}{0.15} = \frac{5.25}{0.15}\left(\frac{100}{100}\right)$$ 0.15 has 2 decimal places, so multiply both numbers

by $\boxed{}$ to make the divisor an integer.

$$= \boxed{}$$ Then divide as with whole numbers.

$$= \boxed{}$$

Example 4

PROBLEM SOLVING APPLICATION

A muffin recipe calls for $\frac{1}{2}$ cup of oats. You have $\frac{3}{4}$ cup of oats. How many batches of muffins can you bake?

1. **Understand the Problem**
   The number of batches of muffins you can bake is the number of batches using the oats that you have. List the important information:

   • The amount of oats is cup.

   • One batch of muffins calls for cup of oats.

2. **Make a Plan**
   Set up an equation.

amount of oats you have	÷	amount for one batch	=	number of batches

Holt Mathematics

3. Solve
Let n = number of batches.

$$\frac{3}{4} \div \frac{1}{2} = n$$

$$\frac{3}{4} \cdot \boxed{} = n$$

$\frac{6}{4}$, or $\boxed{}$ batches of muffins.

4. Look Back
One cup of oats would make $\boxed{}$ batches so $1\frac{1}{2}$ is a

$\boxed{}$ answer.

Check It Out!

1. Divide. Write the answer in simplest form.

$$4\frac{2}{5} \div 3$$

2. Find. 0.65 ÷ 0.25.

3. Evaluate.

$\frac{3.60}{n}$ for $n = 0.12$

4. A ship will use $\frac{1}{6}$ of its total fuel load for a typical round trip. If there is $\frac{5}{8}$ of a total fuel load on board now, how many complete trips can be made?

Holt Mathematics

LESSON 2-6 # Adding and Subtracting with Unlike Denominators

Lesson Objectives

Add and subtract fractions with unlike demoninators

Additional Examples

Example 1

Add or subtract.

Method 1:

A. $\frac{1}{8} + \frac{2}{7}$

Find a common [   ]:

$8(7) = $ [   ].

$= \frac{1}{8}\left(\boxed{}\right) + \frac{2}{7}\left(\boxed{}\right)$ Multiply by fractions equal to [   ].

$= \boxed{} + \boxed{}$ Rewrite with a common [   ].

$= \boxed{}$ Simplify.

Method 2:

B. $1\frac{1}{6} - 1\frac{5}{8}$

$= \boxed{} - \frac{13}{8}$ Write as an [   ] fraction.

Multiples of 6: 6; 12; 24; 30   List the [   ] of each

Multiples of 8: 8; 16; 24; 32   denominator and find the [   ].

$= \frac{7}{6}\boxed{} - \frac{13}{8}\boxed{}$ Multiply by fractions equal to [   ].

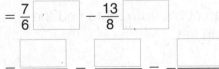

$= \dfrac{\boxed{}}{24} - \dfrac{\boxed{}}{24} = -\dfrac{\boxed{}}{24}$ Rewrite with the [   ].

$= \boxed{}$ Simplify.

Holt Mathematics

Example 2

Find $\frac{25}{56} + \frac{37}{84}$. Write the answer in simplest form.

Factors of 56: □ · □ · □ · □   Write the □
                                  of each denominator.

Factors of 84: □ · □ · □ · □   Circle the common □.

□ , □ , □ , □ , □   List all the □
                      using the circled factors only once.

□ · □ · □ · □ = □   Multiply.

The LCD is □.

168 ÷ 56 = □   168 ÷ 84 = □

$= \frac{25}{56}\left(\square\right) + \frac{37}{84}\left(\square\right)$ Multiply by fractions equal to 1 to get
                                                                              a □.

$= \dfrac{\square}{168} + \dfrac{\square}{168}$ Rewrite using the □.

$= \boxed{}$ Add.

Example 3

Two dancers are making necklaces from ribbon for their costumes. They need pieces measuring $13\frac{3}{4}$ inches and $12\frac{7}{8}$ inches. How much ribbon will be left over after the pieces are cut from a 36-inch length?

$36 - 12\frac{7}{8} - 13\frac{3}{4}$ Subtract both amounts from 36 to find the amount of ribbon left.

$= \dfrac{36}{\square} - \dfrac{\square}{8} - \dfrac{\square}{4}$ Write as improper fractions.

$= \dfrac{\square}{8} - \dfrac{103}{8} - \dfrac{\square}{8}$ The LCD is 8. Simplify.

$= \square$, or $\square$ There will be □ inches left.

Holt Mathematics

Example 4

Evaluate $t - \frac{4}{5}$ for $t = \frac{5}{6}$.

$t - \frac{4}{5}$

$= \boxed{} - \frac{4}{5}$ Substitute $\boxed{}$ for t.

$= \frac{5}{6}\boxed{} - \frac{4}{5}\boxed{}$ Multiply by fractions equal to $\boxed{}$.

$= \boxed{} - \boxed{}$ Rewrite with a $\boxed{}$ denominator:

$6(5) = \boxed{}$.

$= \boxed{}$ Simplify.

Check It Out!

1. Add.

$2\frac{1}{6} + \frac{3}{4}$

2. Find $\frac{19}{32} + \frac{9}{80}$. Write the answer in simplest form.

3. Fred and Jose are building a tree house. They need to cut a $6\frac{3}{4}$ foot piece of wood and a $4\frac{5}{12}$ foot piece of wood from a 12 foot board. How much of the board will be left?

4. Evaluate $\frac{5}{9} - h$ for $h = \frac{-7}{12}$.

Holt Mathematics

LESSON 2-7 One-Step Equations with Rational Numbers

Know it! .Note

Lesson Objectives

Solve one-step equations with rational numbers

Additional Examples

Example 1

Solve.

A. $m + 4.6 = 9$

$m + 4.6 = 9$

$-\boxed{} = -\boxed{}$ Since 4.6 is added to m, subtract $\boxed{}$

$m = \boxed{}$ from both sides to undo the addition.

B. $8.2p = -32.8$

$\dfrac{8.2p}{\boxed{}} = \dfrac{-32.8}{\boxed{}}$ Since p is multiplied by 8.2, divide both

sides by $\boxed{}$ to undo the

$p = \boxed{}$ multiplication.

C. $\dfrac{x}{1.2} = 15$

$\boxed{} \cdot \dfrac{x}{1.2} = \boxed{} \cdot 15$ Since x is divided by 1.2, multiply both

$x = \boxed{}$ sides by $\boxed{}$ to undo the division.

Example 2

Solve.

A. $y - \dfrac{1}{6} = \dfrac{2}{3}$

$\boxed{} + y - \dfrac{1}{6} = \dfrac{2}{3} + \boxed{}$ Since $\dfrac{1}{6}$ is subtracted from y, add $\boxed{}$ to both sides to undo the subtraction.

$y = \dfrac{\boxed{}}{6} + \dfrac{\boxed{}}{6}$ Find a common $\boxed{}$; 6.

$y = \boxed{}$ Simplify.

Holt Mathematics

B. $\frac{5}{6}x = \frac{5}{8}$

$\frac{5}{6}x \div \frac{5}{6} = \frac{5}{8} \div \frac{5}{6}$

$\frac{1\cancel{5}}{1\cancel{6}}x \cdot \frac{\cancel{6}^1}{\cancel{5}_1} = \frac{1\cancel{5}}{8} \cdot \frac{6}{\cancel{5}_1}$

$x = \boxed{}$

Since x is multiplied by $\frac{5}{6}$, divide both sides by $\frac{5}{6}$.

Multiply by the $\boxed{}$.

Simplify.

Example 3

Janice has saved $21.40. This is $\frac{1}{3}$ of what she needs to save to buy a new piece of software. What is the total amount that Janis needs to save?

Write an equation:

total amount needed $\cdot \frac{1}{3}$ = **amount Janis has saved**

$a \qquad \cdot \frac{1}{3} = \qquad \$21.40$

$a \cdot \frac{1}{3} \div \boxed{} = 21.40 \div \boxed{}$

Since a is multiplied by $\frac{1}{3}$, divide both sides by $\boxed{}$.

$a \cdot \frac{1}{3} \cdot \boxed{} = 21.40 \cdot \boxed{}$

Multiply by the $\boxed{}$.

$a = \boxed{}$

Janet needs to save a total of $\boxed{}$.

Check It Out!

1. $m + 9.1 = 3$

2. $\frac{3}{8}x = \frac{3}{4}$

3. Rick's car holds $\frac{2}{3}$ the amount of gasoline as his wife's van. If the car's gas tank hold 24 gallons of gasoline, how much gasoline can the tank in the minivan hold?

California Standards ← AF4.1

LESSON 2-8 **Two-Step Equations with Rational Numbers**

Lesson Objectives

Solve two-step equations with rational numbers

Additional Examples

Example 1

PROBLEM SOLVING APPLICATION

The mechanic's bill to repair Mr. Wong's car was $653.05. The mechanic charges $45.50 an hour for labor, and the parts that were used cost $443.75. How many hours did the mechanic work on the car?

1. **Understand the Problem**
   List the important information:

   The answer is the number of [ ] the mechanic worked on the car.

   • The parts cost $[ ] .

   • The labor cost $[ ] per hour.

   • The total bill was $[ ] .

   Let *h* represent the hours the mechanic worked.

   Total bill = Parts + Labor

   [ ] = [ ] + [ ] *h*

2. **Make a Plan**
   Think: First the variable is multiplied by [ ] , and then [ ] is

   added to the result. Work backward to solve the equation. Undo the

   operations in reverse order: First subtract [ ] from both sides of

   the equation, and then divide both sides of the new equation by [ ] .

Holt Mathematics

3. Solve

$$\boxed{} = \boxed{} + \boxed{}\,h \qquad \text{Since 443.75 is added to 45.5 } h,$$

$$-\boxed{} \qquad -\boxed{} \qquad \text{subtract } \boxed{} \text{ from both sides.}$$

$$\boxed{} = \boxed{}\,h \qquad \text{Since } h \text{ is multiplied by 45.5,}$$

$$\boxed{} = \boxed{} \qquad \text{divide both sides by } \boxed{}.$$

$$\boxed{} = h$$

The mechanic worked for ⬜ hours on Mr. Wong's car.

4. Look Back

If the mechanic worked ⬜ hours, the labor would be $45.50(4.6) = $209.30.

The sum of the parts and the labor would be $\boxed{}$ +

$\boxed{}$ = $\boxed{}$.

Example 2

Solve.

A. $\dfrac{n}{3} + 7 = 22$

$$\dfrac{n}{3} + 7 = 22 \qquad \text{Since 7 is added to } \dfrac{n}{3},$$

$$-\boxed{} \quad -\boxed{} \qquad \text{subtract } \boxed{} \text{ from both sides to undo the addition.}$$

$$\dfrac{n}{3} = \boxed{} \qquad \text{Since } n \text{ is divided by 3,}$$

$$\boxed{} \cdot \dfrac{n}{3} = \boxed{} \cdot 15 \qquad \text{multiply both sides by } \boxed{} \text{ to undo the division.}$$

$$n = \boxed{}$$

Holt Mathematics

B. $\dfrac{y-4}{3} = 9$

$\dfrac{y-4}{3} = 9$ Since $y - 4$ is divided by 3,

$\boxed{} \cdot \dfrac{y-4}{3} = \boxed{} \cdot 9$ multiply both sides by $\boxed{}$ to undo the division.

$y - 4 = \boxed{}$ Since 4 is subtracted from y,

$\underline{+\ \boxed{}}\quad\underline{+\ \boxed{}}$ add $\boxed{}$ to both sides to undo the subtraction.

$y = \boxed{}$

Check It Out!

1. The mechanic's bill to repair your car was $850. The mechanic charges $35 an hour for labor, and the parts that were used cost $275. How many hours did the mechanic work on your car?

2. Solve.

$\dfrac{n}{4} + 8 = 18$

Holt Mathematics

Chapter Review

2-1 Rational Numbers

Simplify.

1. $\frac{13}{26}$ 2. $\frac{18}{33}$ 3. $\frac{14}{56}$ 4. $\frac{16}{30}$

Write each decimal as a fraction in simplest form.

5. 0.45 6. 1.17 7. −3.04 8. 0.725

2-2 Comparing and Ordering Rational Numbers

Compare. Write $<$, $>$, or $=$.

9. $\frac{5}{6}$ ▆ $\frac{5}{7}$ 10. $-\frac{21}{15}$ ▆ $\frac{14}{11}$ 11. $\frac{13}{8}$ ▆ $\frac{26}{16}$ 12. 6.5 ▆ $6\frac{3}{5}$

13. The lengths of four student's pencils in Mr. Roberson's class are 5.75 inches, 5.8 inches, $5\frac{5}{6}$ inches, and 5.83 inches. List these measurements in order from least to greatest.

2-3 Adding and Subtracting Rational Numbers

Evaluate each expression for the given value of the variable.

14. $74.28 - m$ for $m = 31.72$ 15. $-\frac{2}{3} + t$ for $t = \frac{7}{3}$ 16. $\frac{5}{9} + x$ for $x = -3\frac{4}{9}$

17. Sammie and Lance both jog home after school every day. On Thursday, they made it home in 0.75 hour. Friday, it took them $\frac{3}{5}$ of an hour. How much longer did it take Sammie and Lance to jog home on Thursday than Friday?

2-4 Multiplying Rational Numbers

Multiply. Write each answer in simplest form.

18. $2\frac{3}{7}\left(\frac{4}{5}\right)$ 19. $3.4(6.7)$ 20. $-\frac{1}{4}\left(\frac{5}{6}\right)$ 21. $-7.2(-9.1)$

22. Kylie needs to cut 6 pieces of yarn that are each $\frac{2}{3}$ foot long. How much yarn does Kylie need?

 Holt Mathematics

2-5 Dividing Rational Numbers

Divide. Write each answer in simplest form.

23. $\frac{7}{9} \div \frac{2}{3}$

24. $-\frac{2}{7} \div \frac{6}{5}$

25. $\frac{3}{4} \div -2$

Evaluate each expression for the given value of the variable.

26. $\frac{8.6}{h}$ for $h = 0.4$

27. $\frac{17.8}{p}$ for $p = 2$

28. $\frac{59.22}{l}$ for $l = 4.7$

2-6 Adding and Subtracting with Unlike Demoninators

Add or Subtract.

29. $\frac{1}{9} + \frac{4}{5}$

30. $\frac{6}{7} - \frac{1}{3}$

31. $3\frac{1}{4} + 1\frac{1}{6}$

32. $5\frac{5}{8} - 3\frac{1}{2}$

33. Sallie needs $4\frac{1}{4}$ cup of milk for a recipe. She has $2\frac{2}{3}$ cups of milk. How much more milk does Sallie need?

2-7 One-Step Equations with Rational Numbers

Solve.

34. $-7.1 - y = 3.7$ **35.** $62.3 + g = 80.9$ **36.** $\frac{s}{4.6} = 11.4$ **37.** $w + \frac{6}{11} = \frac{1}{3}$

38. Amy watched television for $2\frac{3}{4}$ hours. Charles watched television for $\frac{1}{3}$ of the time Amy did. How long, in minutes, did Charles watch television?

2-8 Two-Step Equations with Rational Numbers

Solve.

39. $3d + 7.3 = 31$ **40.** $\frac{c-9}{4} = -6$ **41.** $12 + \frac{v}{2} = 17$ **42.** $\frac{1}{3}u + \frac{3}{4} = \frac{1}{6}$

43. Gina bought a magazine subscription. The magazine company charged $15.75 for the subscription and $2.15 for each issue. If Gina paid $45.85, how many issues did she receive?

Holt Mathematics

Big Ideas

Answer these question to summarize the important concepts from Chapter 2 in your own words.

1. Explain how to write −2.54 as a fraction in simplest terms.

2. Explain how to add $\frac{4}{9}$ and $\frac{2}{9}$.

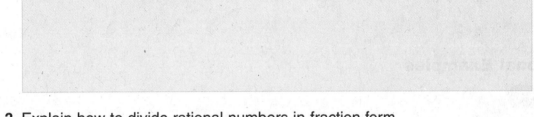

3. Explain how to divide rational numbers in fraction form.

4. Explain how to solve the equation $x - \frac{1}{5} = \frac{4}{15}$.

For more review of Chapter 2:

- Complete the Chapter 2 Study Guide and Review on pages 106–108 of your textbook.

- Complete the Ready to Go On quizzes on pages 92 and 102 of your textbook.

Holt Mathematics

LESSON 3-1 **Properties of Rational Numbers**

Lesson Objectives

Identify properties of rational numbers and use them to simplify numerical expressions

Vocabulary

Commutative Property (p. 116) _____

_____

Associative Property (p. 116) _____

_____

Distributive Property (p. 117) _____

_____

Additional Examples

Example 1

Name the property that is illustrated in each equation.

A. $(-4) \cdot 9 = 9 \cdot (-4)$ The [_____] of the factors has changed.

B. $\left(5 + \frac{3}{4}\right) + \frac{1}{4} = 5 + \left(\frac{3}{4} + \frac{1}{4}\right)$ The numbers are [_____] differently.

Holt Mathematics

Example 2

Simplify each expression. Justify each step.

A. $29 + 37 + 1$

$29 + 37 + 1 = \boxed{} + \boxed{} + 1$ Commutative Property of Addition

$= 37 + (29 + 1)$ Associative Property of Addition

$= 37 + \boxed{}$ Add.

$= \boxed{}$

B. $7 \cdot \dfrac{2}{9} \cdot \dfrac{1}{7}$

$7 \cdot \dfrac{2}{9} \cdot \dfrac{1}{7} = 7 \cdot \boxed{} \cdot \boxed{}$ Commutative Property of Multiplication

$= \left(7 \cdot \dfrac{1}{7}\right) \cdot \dfrac{2}{9}$ Associative Property of Multiplication

$= \boxed{} \cdot \dfrac{2}{9}$ Multiply.

$= \boxed{}$

Example 3

Write each product using the Distributive Property. Then simplify.

A. $9(31)$

$9(31) = 9(\boxed{})$ Rewrite 31 as a $\boxed{}$.

$= 9 \cdot 30 + 9 \cdot 1$ Distributive Property

$= 270 + 9$ Multiply.

$= \boxed{}$ Add.

B. $8(59)$

$8(59) = 8(\boxed{})$ Rewrite 59 as a $\boxed{}$.

$= 8 \cdot 60 - 8 \cdot 1$ Distributive Property

$= 480 - 8$ Multiply.

$= \boxed{}$ Subtract.

Holt Mathematics

Check It Out!

1. Name the property that is illustrated in the equation.

$(18 + 4) + 6 = 18 + (4 + 6)$

2. Simplify the expression. Justify each step.

$4 \cdot 3 \cdot \frac{1}{4}$

3. Write the product using the Distributive Property: 8(19). Then simplify.

Holt Mathematics

Simplifying Algebraic Expressions

Lesson Objectives

Combine like terms in an expression

Vocabulary

term (p. 120) _____

_____

like term (p. 120) _____

_____

coefficient (p. 120) _____

_____

constant (p. 120) _____

_____

equivalent expression (p. 120) _____

_____

Additional Examples

Example 1

Combine like terms.

$14a - 5a$

$14a - 5a$ Identify [   ] terms.

[   ]   Combine coefficients: [   ] − [   ] = [   ]

Example 2

Combine like terms.

$9x + 3y - 2x + 5$

$9x + 3y - 2x + 5$ Identify [   ] terms.

$9x - 2x + 3y + 5$ Commutative Property.

[   ]   Combine coefficients: [   ] − [   ] = 7

57   **Holt Mathematics**

Example 3

Simplify 6(5 + *n*) − 2*n*.

6(5 + *n*) − 2*n*

6(5) + 6(*n*) − 2*n*   [ ] Property

30 + 6*n* − 2*n*   Identify [ ] terms.

[ ] + [ ]*n*   Combine coefficients: 6 − 2 = [ ]

Check It Out!

1. Combine like terms.

5*c* + 8 − 4*c* − 2 − *c*

2. Combine like terms.

9*d* + 7*c* − 4*d* − 2*c*

3. Simplify 3(*c* + 7) − *c*.

Holt Mathematics

LESSON 3-3

Solving Multi-Step Equations

Know it! Note

Lesson Objectives

Solve multi-step equations

Additional Examples

Example 1

Solve.

$8x + 6 + 3x - 2 = 37$

$8x + 3x + 6 - 2 = 37$ Commutative Property of Addition

$\boxed{}\,x + \boxed{} = 37$ Combine like terms.

$-4 \quad -4$ Since $\boxed{}$ is added to $\boxed{}\,x$, subtract $\boxed{}$

$\boxed{}\,x = 33$ from both sides to undo the $\boxed{}$.

$\dfrac{11x}{11} = \dfrac{33}{11}$ Since x is multiplied by 11, $\boxed{}$ both

$x = \boxed{}$ sides by $\boxed{}$ to undo the multiplication.

Example 2

Solve.

$\dfrac{5n}{4} + \dfrac{7}{4} = \dfrac{-3}{4}$

$\boxed{}\left(\dfrac{5n}{4} + \dfrac{7}{4}\right) = \boxed{}\left(\dfrac{-3}{4}\right)$ Multiply both sides by 4.

$4\left(\dfrac{5n}{4}\right) + 4\left(\dfrac{7}{4}\right) = 4\left(\dfrac{-3}{4}\right)$ $\boxed{}$ Property

$\boxed{}\,n + \boxed{} = \boxed{}$ Since $\boxed{}$ is added to $\boxed{}\,n$, $\boxed{}$ 7 from both sides to undo the addition.

$-7 \quad -7$

$\boxed{}\,n = \boxed{}$ Since n is multiplied by 5, divide both sides by

$\dfrac{5n}{5} = \dfrac{-10}{5}$ $\boxed{}$ to undo the $\boxed{}$.

$n = \boxed{}$

Holt Mathematics

Example 3

On Monday, David rides his bicycle *m* miles in 2 hours. On Tuesday, he rides three times as far in 5 hours. If his average speed for the two days is 12 mi/h, how far did he ride on Monday, to the nearest tenth of a mile?

David's average speed is his total distance for the two days divided by the total time.

$$\frac{\text{Total distance}}{\text{Total time}} = \text{average speed}$$

$$\frac{m + 3m}{\boxed{}} = 12$$ Substitute $m + 3m$ for total distance

and $\boxed{}$ for total time.

$$\frac{4m}{7} = 12$$ Simplify.

$$\boxed{}\left(\frac{4m}{7}\right) = \boxed{}(12)$$ Multiply both sides by $\boxed{}$.

$$4m = 84$$

$$\frac{4m}{\boxed{}} = \frac{84}{\boxed{}}$$ Divide by sides by $\boxed{}$.

David rode $\boxed{}$ miles on Monday.

Check It Out!

1. Solve.

$$9x + 5 + 4x - 2 = 42$$

2. Solve.

$$\frac{5x}{9} + \frac{x}{3} - \frac{13}{9} = \frac{1}{3}$$

3. On Saturday, Penelope rode her scooter *m* miles in 3 hours. On Sunday, she rides twice as far in 7 hours. If her average speed for the two days is 20 mi/h, how far did she ride on Saturday to the nearest tenth of a mile?

Holt Mathematics

LESSON 3-4 Solving Equations with Variables on Both Sides

Lesson Objectives

Solve equations with variables on both sides of the equal sign

Additional Examples

Solve.

$$4x + 6 = x$$

$$\underline{-\boxed{}} \qquad \underline{-\boxed{}}$$

$$6 = \boxed{}\, x$$

To collect the variable terms on one side, subtract $\boxed{}$ from both sides.

$$\frac{6}{\boxed{}} = \frac{-3x}{\boxed{}}$$

Since x is multiplied by -3, divide both sides by $\boxed{}$.

$$\boxed{} = x$$

Example 2

Solve.

$$10z - 15 - 4z = 8 - 2z - 15$$

$$\boxed{} - 15 = -2z - \boxed{}$$

Combine like terms.

$$+\,\boxed{} \qquad +\,\boxed{}$$

$$\boxed{} - 15 = -7$$

To collect the variable terms on one side, add $\boxed{}$ to both sides.

$$+\,\boxed{} \qquad +\,\boxed{}$$

Since 15 is subtracted from $\boxed{}$, add $\boxed{}$ to both sides.

$$8z = \boxed{}$$

$$\frac{8z}{\boxed{}} = \frac{8}{\boxed{}}$$

Since z is multiplied by 8, divide both sides by $\boxed{}$.

$$z = \boxed{}$$

Holt Mathematics

Example 3

Daisy's Flowers sells a rose bouquet for $39.95 plus $2.95 for every rose. A competing florist sells a similar bouquet for $26.00 plus $4.50 for every rose. Find the number of roses that would make both florists' bouquets cost the same price. What is the price?

Write an equation for each florist's bouquet. Let *r* represent the number of roses and *c* represent the total cost.

	total cost	is	bouquet cost	plus	cost	per rose
Daisy's Flowers:	*c*	=	39.95	+	2.95	*r*
competing florist:	*c*	=	26.00	+	4.50	*r*

Now write an equation showing that the costs are equal.

$39.95 + 2.95r = 26.00 + 4.50r$

$$- \boxed{} = - \boxed{}$$

To collect the variable terms on one side,

$39.95 \quad = \quad 26.00 + 1.55r$ subtract $\boxed{}$ from both sides.

$$- \boxed{} = - \boxed{}$$

Subtract $\boxed{}$ from both sides.

$13.95 \quad = \quad 1.55r$

$$\frac{13.95}{\boxed{}} = \frac{1.55r}{\boxed{}}$$

Divide both sides by $\boxed{}$.

 $= r$

The two florists charge the same for a bouquet with $\boxed{}$ roses.

To find the cost, substitute $\boxed{}$ for *r* in either equation.

Daisy's Flowers:

$c = 39.95 + 2.95r$

$= 39.95 + 2.95(\underline{})$

$= 39.95 + \boxed{}$

$= \boxed{}$

competing florist

$c = 26.00 + 4.50r$

$= 26.00 + 4.50(\underline{})$

$= 26.00 + \boxed{}$

$= \boxed{}$

The cost for a bouquet with 9 roses from either florist is $\boxed{}$

Holt Mathematics

Check It Out!

1. Solve.

    $3b - 2 = 2b + 12$

2. Solve.

    $12z - 12 - 4z = 6 - 2z + 32$

3. Marla's Gift Baskets sell a muffin basket for $22.00 plus $2.25 for every balloon. A competing service sells a similar muffin basket for $16.00 plus $3.00 for every balloon. Find the number of balloons that would make both baskets cost the same price.

Holt Mathematics

LESSON 3-5 Inequalities

Lesson Objectives

Write inequalities that represent verbal descriptions and graph inequalities on a number line

Vocabulary

inequality (p. 136) _____

_____

algebraic inequality (p. 136) _____

_____

solution set (p. 137) _____

_____

Additional Examples

Example 1

Write an inequality for the situation.

There are at least 35 people in the gym.

[   ]

"At least" means

[   ] than or

[   ] to.

Example 2

Write an inequality for the statement.

A number m multiplied by 5 is less than 25.

A number m multiplied by 5 is less than 25.

m •   5   <   25

[   ]

Holt Mathematics

Example 3

Graph the inequality.

$-1 > y$

Example 4

Write a compound inequality for each statement.

A number x is both less than 4 and greater than or equal to -2.5.

$-2.5 \le x < 4$

Check It Out!

1. Write an inequality for the situation.

There are at most 10 gallons of gas in the tank.

2. Write an inequality for the statement.

A number y plus 14 is greater than 21.

3. Graph the inequality.

$p \le 2$

4. Write a compound inequality for the statement.

A number y is either greater than -5 or less than or equal to -1.

Holt Mathematics

LESSON 3-6 Solving Inequalities by Adding or Subtracting

Lesson Objectives

Solve one-step inequalities by using addition or subtraction

Additional Examples

Example 1

Solve and graph each inequality.

A. $x + 3 > -5$

Subtract ☐ from both sides.

$x >$ ☐

−9 −8 −7 −6 −5 −4 −3 −2 −1 0 1

B. $m - 4 \geq -2$

Add ☐ to both sides.

$m \geq$ ☐

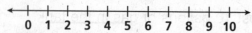
0 1 2 3 4 5 6 7 8 9 10

C. $r + 3 \leq -3$

Subtract ☐ from both sides.

$c \leq$ ☐

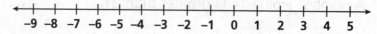
−9 −8 −7 −6 −5 −4 −3 −2 −1 0 1 2 3 4 5

D. $5\frac{3}{4} > n + 1\frac{1}{4}$

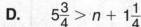

Subtract ☐ from both sides.

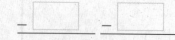
☐ $> n$

−7 −6 −5 −4 −3 −2 −1 0 1 2 3 4 5 6 7

Holt Mathematics

Example 2

While training for a race, Ann's goal is to run at least 3.5 miles each day. She has already run 1.8 miles today. Write and solve an inequality to find out how many more miles she must run today.

Let m = the number of additional miles.

1.8 miles	plus	additional miles	is at least	3.5 miles
1.8	+	m	☐	3.5

$1.8 + m \geq 3.5$ Since ☐ is added to m, subtract ☐

$-$☐ $-$☐   from both sides.

$m \geq$ ☐

Ann should run at least ☐ more miles.

Check It Out!

Solve and graph the inequality.

1. $3\frac{2}{3} > n + 1\frac{1}{3}$

2. **Tim's company produces recycled paper. They produce 60.5 lbs of paper each day. They have already produced at least 20.2 lbs today. Write and solve an inequality to find out how many more pounds Tim's company must produce.**

67

Holt Mathematics

California Standards ← AF4.1, AF1.1

LESSON 3-7 Solving Inequalities by Multiplying or Dividing

Lesson Objectives

Solve one-step inequalities by using multiplication or division

Additional Examples

Example 1

Solve and graph.

A. $12 < \dfrac{a}{4}$

$\boxed{} \cdot 12 < \boxed{} \cdot \dfrac{a}{4}$ Multiply both sides by $\boxed{}$.

$\boxed{}$, or $\boxed{}$

number line: 43 44 45 46 47 48 49 50 51 52

Check

According to the graph, 49 should be a solution because 49 > 48, and 47 should not be a solution because 47 < 48.

$12 \underset{?}{<} \dfrac{a}{4}$ $12 \underset{?}{<} \dfrac{a}{4}$

$12 < \dfrac{49}{4}$ Substitute 49 for a. $12 < \dfrac{47}{4}$ Substitute 47 for a.

$12 < \boxed{}$ √ $12 < \boxed{}$ x

So 49 $\boxed{}$ a solution.   So 47 $\boxed{}$ a solution.

Example 2

A rock-collecting club needs at least $500. They buy rocks for $2.50 and sell them for $4.00. What is the least number of rocks the club must sell?

1. **Understand the Problem**
   The answer is the number of rocks the rock-collecting club must sell to make at least $500. List the important information:

   • The rock-collecting club needs to make at least $ $\boxed{}$.

   • They are buying rocks for $ $\boxed{}$, and selling rocks for $ $\boxed{}$.

   Show the relationship of the information:

   (the price for selling a rock – the price for buying a rock) • the number of rocks sold ≥ $500

Holt Mathematics

2. Make a Plan

Write an inequality. Let *x* represent the number of rocks sold.

($\boxed{}$ − $\boxed{}$) · $x \geq$ $500

3. Solve

($4.00 − $2.50) · $x \geq$ $500

$1.50 · $x \geq$ $500

$$\frac{\$1.50x}{\$\boxed{}} \geq \frac{\$500}{\$\boxed{}}$$ Divide both sides by $\boxed{}$.

$x \geq \boxed{}$ At least $\boxed{}$ rocks must be sold.

4. Look Back

Selling 334 rocks would make $1.50 · 334 = $ $\boxed{}$.

Check It Out!

Solve and graph the inequality.

1. $16 > \dfrac{b}{5}$

2. The music club needs to make at least 3 times more than the language club made ($132) in order to go to the symphony. They are selling music sheet holders for $3.75. What is the least number of music sheet holders the club must sell to make the goal?

Holt Mathematics

Solving Two-Step Inequalities

LESSON 3-8

Lesson Objectives

Solve two-step inequalities and graph the solutions of an inequality on a number line

Additional Examples

Solve and graph.

A. $4x + 1 > 13$

$$4x + 1 > 13$$

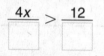   Subtract ☐ from both sides.

$$4x > \boxed{}$$

$$\frac{4x}{\boxed{}} > \frac{12}{\boxed{}}$$ Divide both sides by ☐.

$$x > \boxed{}$$

B. $-9x + 7 \geq 25$

$$-9x + 7 \geq 25$$

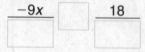   Subtract ☐ from both sides.

$$-9x \geq \boxed{}$$

$$\frac{-9x}{\boxed{}} \; \boxed{} \; \frac{18}{\boxed{}}$$ 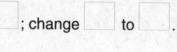 Divide both sides by ☐; change ☐ to ☐.

$$x \; \boxed{} \; \boxed{}$$

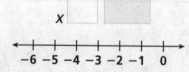

Holt Mathematics

Example 2

Solve $\frac{2x}{5} + \frac{3}{4} \geq \frac{9}{10}$ and graph the solution.

$$\boxed{}\left(\frac{2x}{5} + \frac{3}{4}\right) \geq \boxed{}\left(\frac{9}{10}\right)$$ Multiply by the LCD, $\boxed{}$.

$$\boxed{}\left(\frac{2x}{5}\right) + \boxed{}\left(\frac{3}{4}\right) \geq \boxed{}\left(\frac{9}{10}\right)$$ Distributive Property

$$\boxed{} + \boxed{} \geq \boxed{}$$ Combine like terms.

$$-\boxed{} \quad -\boxed{}$$ Subtract $\boxed{}$ from both sides.

$$\boxed{} \geq \boxed{}$$

$$\frac{8x}{\boxed{}} \geq \frac{3}{\boxed{}}$$ Divide both sides by $\boxed{}$.

$$x \geq \boxed{}$$

Example 3

A school's Spanish club is selling bumper stickers. They bought 100 stickers for $55 and have to give the company 15 cents for every sticker that the club sells. If they plan to sell each bumper sticker for $1.25, how many do they have to sell to make a profit?

To make a profit, bumper sticker sales must be greater than the cost of the stickers, plus the amount per sticker sold given to the company.

Let s represent the total number of stickers sold.

$$1.25s > 55 + (0.15s)$$

$$-\boxed{} \qquad -\boxed{}$$ Subtract $\boxed{}$ from both sides.

$$1.1s > 55$$

$$\frac{1.1s}{\boxed{}} > \frac{55}{\boxed{}}$$ Divide both sides by $\boxed{}$.

$$s > \boxed{}$$

To make a profit, the club needs to sell more than $\boxed{}$ bumper stickers.

Holt Mathematics

Check It Out!

1. Solve and graph.

$-4x + 2 \geq 18$

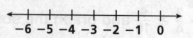

2. Solve and graph.

$\dfrac{3x}{5} + \dfrac{1}{4} \geq \dfrac{5}{10}$

3. A school's French club is selling bumper stickers. They bought 200 bumper stickers for $45, and they have to give the company 25 cents for every sticker sold. If they plan to sell each bumper sticker for $2.50, how many do they have to sell to make a profit?

Holt Mathematics

Chapter Review

3-1 Properties of Rational Numbers

Name the property that is illustrated in each equation.

1. $2 \cdot (4 \cdot 3) = (2 \cdot 4) \cdot 3$ **2.** $7 + 5 = 5 + 7$ **3.** $5(4 - 3) = 5$

Write each product using the Distributive Property. Then simplify.

4. $5(18) =$ **5.** $(22)2 =$

3-2 Simplifying Algebraic Expressions

Combine like terms.

6. $6b + 11b$ **7.** $8c + 4 - 3c$ **8.** $5p + 7 - 3p - 2 + 6p$

9. $7t + 4w + 8 - t$ **10.** $9f + 6g - 4f - 2g + 2$ **11.** $14u + 5w + 4 - 3u + 4w$

3-3 Solving Multi-Step Equations

Solve.

12. $6t + 5t - 2t + 8 = 71$ **13.** $-53 = 5f + 8f + 12$

14. $42 - 4s - 7s = 207$ **15.** $\dfrac{15j}{28} - \dfrac{9j}{14} = \dfrac{9}{7}$

16. The sum of two consecutive even numbers is 74. What are the two numbers? Explain your solution.

Holt Mathematics

3-4 Solving Equations with Variables on Both Sides

Solve and check.

17. $7e + 9 = 9e - 3$

18. $18v - 2 = -8 + 21v$

19. $4(3z + 10) = 5z - 9$

20. $3(2x - 5) - 15 = 4x + 3.2 - 8x$

21. $\frac{1}{4}(4b + 12) = 7b - 12 - b$

22. $\frac{d}{24} + 3.5 + 4d = \frac{5}{12} - \frac{7d}{24} + \frac{11}{12}$

3-5 Inequalities

Write an inequality for each situation.

23. There are no more than 25 students in each class.

24. The height of that cliff is at least 500 feet.

Graph each inequality.

25. $x \leq -2$

26. $x < 3$

27. $y \leq 7$

3-6 Solving Inequalities by Adding or Subtracting

Compare. Write < or >.

28. $8(-2)$ ▨ 15

29. $-14 - (-8)$ ▨ -5

30. $7 - 18$ ▨ -12

Solve.

31. $k - 13 < 5$

32. $6 + z \geq 32$

33. $j - 18 > -10$

34. The band members need to raise $1,523 for their new uniforms. So far they have raised $978. At least how much money must the band members raise in order to purchase their new uniforms?

Holt Mathematics

3-7 Solving Inequalities by Multiplying or Dividing

Write and solve an algebraic inequality.

35. Five times a number is greater than 65.

36. The quotient of some number and 6 is less than 20.

37. The product of -8 and a number is at least 88.

38. Nicole can save $5.50 of her weekly allowance. To save $48 for a concert ticket, what is the least number of weeks that she must save her allowance?

3-8 Solving Two-Step Inequalities

Solve and graph.

39. $2j + 14 \le -26$ 40. $11 - 9p \le 92$ 41. $8k + 15 > 19$

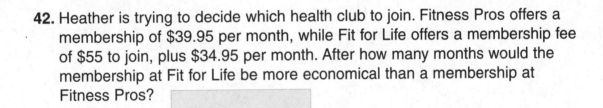

42. Heather is trying to decide which health club to join. Fitness Pros offers a membership of $39.95 per month, while Fit for Life offers a membership fee of $55 to join, plus $34.95 per month. After how many months would the membership at Fit for Life be more economical than a membership at Fitness Pros?

Holt Mathematics

Big Ideas

Answer these questions to summarize the important concepts from Chapter 3 in your own words.

1. Explain how to simplify the expression $4(7x - 3) + 2x$.

2. Explain how to solve the equation $6x + 10 + 12x - 14 = 50$.

3. Explain how to solve the equation $4b + 8 - 6b = -18 + 2b + 10$.

4. Explain how to solve the inequality $12 \leq \dfrac{c}{-5}$.

5. Explain what an open circle and a closed circle mean when graphing inequalities on a number line.

For more review of Chapter 3:

• Complete the Chapter 3 Study Guide and Review on pages 186–189 of your textbook.

• Complete the Ready to Go On quizzes on pages 155 and 185 of your textbook.

Holt Mathematics

Exponents

Lesson Objectives

Simplify expressions with exponents

Vocabulary

exponential form (p. 168) _____

_____

exponent (p. 168) _____

_____

base (p. 168) _____

_____

power (p. 168) _____

_____

Additional Examples

Example 1

Write in exponential form.

A. $4 \cdot 4 \cdot 4 \cdot 4$

$4 \cdot 4 \cdot 4 \cdot 4 = $ [____]   Identify how many times [__] is a factor.

B. $(-6) \cdot (-6) \cdot (-6)$

$(-6) \cdot (-6) \cdot (-6) = $ [_____]   Identify how many times (-6) is a

[_____].

C. $5 \cdot 5 \cdot d \cdot d \cdot d \cdot d$

$5 \cdot 5 \cdot d \cdot d \cdot d \cdot d = $ [_____]   Identify how many times [__] and

[__] are each used as a factor.

Example 2

Simplify.

A. 3^5

$3^5 = $ [_____]   Find the product.

$= $ [____]

B. $\left(\dfrac{1}{3}\right)^3$

$\left(\dfrac{1}{3}\right)^3 = $ [_____]   Find the product.

$= $ [____]

C. $(-4)^4$

$(-4)^4 = $ [_____]   Find the product.

$= $ [____]

Example 3

Evaluate $x(y^x - z^y) + x^y$ for $x = 4$, $y = 2$, and $z = 3$.

$x(y^x - z^y) + x^y$

$4(2^4 - 3^2) + 4^2$ Substitute [__] for x, [__] for y, and [__] for z.

$= 4($ [__] $-$ [__] $) + $ [__]   Simplify the [_____].

$= 4($ [__] $) + 16$ [_____] inside the parentheses.

$= $ [__] $+ 16$ [_____] from left to right.

$= $ [__]   [_____].

Holt Mathematics

Example 4

Use the expression $\frac{1}{2}(n^2 - 3n)$ to find the number of diagonals in a 7-sided figure.

$\frac{1}{2}(n^2 - 3n)$

$\frac{1}{2}(7^2 - 3 \cdot 7)$ Substitute the number of sides for n.

$\frac{1}{2}(\boxed{} - \boxed{})$ Simplify inside the $\boxed{}$.

$\frac{1}{2}(\boxed{})$ $\boxed{}$ inside the parentheses.

$\boxed{}$ diagonals $\boxed{}$.

Check It Out!

1. Write in exponential form.

$7 \cdot 7 \cdot b \cdot b$

2. Evaluate.

-9^4

3. Evaluate $z - 7(2^x - x^y)$ **for** $x = 5$, $y = 2$, **and** $z = 60$.

4. Use the expression $\frac{1}{2}(n^2 - 3n)$ **to find the number of diagonals in a 4-sided figure.**

Holt Mathematics

LESSON 4-2 # Integer Exponents

Lesson Objectives

Simplify expressions with negative exponents and the zero exponent

Additional Examples

Example 1

Simplify the powers of 10.

A. 10^{-2}

$10^{-2} = \dfrac{1}{10 \cdot 10}$ Extend the pattern from the table.

$10^{-2} = \boxed{} = \boxed{}$ Multiply. Write as a decimal.

B. 10^{-1}

$10^{-1} = \dfrac{1}{10}$ Extend the pattern from the table.

$10^{-1} = \boxed{} = \boxed{}$ Write as a decimal.

Example 2

Simplify.

A. 5^{-3}

$\dfrac{1}{5^3}$ Write the $\boxed{}$ under 1; change the $\boxed{}$ of the exponent.

$\dfrac{1}{5 \cdot 5 \cdot 5}$ Find the product.

$\boxed{}$ Simplify.

B. $(-10)^{-3}$

$= \dfrac{1}{(-10)^3}$ Write the $\boxed{}$ under 1; change the $\boxed{}$ of the exponent.

$= \dfrac{1}{(-10) \cdot (-10) \cdot (-10)}$ Find the product.

$= \boxed{} = \boxed{}$ Simplify. Write as a decimal.

Holt Mathematics

Example 3

Simplify $5 - (6 - 4)^{-3} + (-2)^0$.

$5 - (6 - 4)^{-3} + (-2)^0$

$= 5 - (\boxed{})^{-3} + (-2)^0$ Subtract inside the $\boxed{}$.

$= 5 - (\boxed{}) + (-2)^0$ Rewrite 2^{-3}.

$= 5 - (\boxed{}) + 1$ Simplify the $\boxed{}$.

$= \boxed{}$ Add and subtract from left to right.

Check It Out!

1. Simplify the power of 10.

10^{-8}

2. Simplify $(-4)^{-2}$.

3. Simplify $3 + (7 - 4)^{-2} + (-8)^0$.

Holt Mathematics

LESSON 4-3

Properties of Exponents

Lesson Objectives

Apply the properties of exponents

Additional Examples

Example 1

Simplify each expression. Write your answer in exponential form.

A. $6^6 \cdot 6^3$

☐ ☐ exponents.

☐

B. $n^5 \cdot n^7$

☐ ☐ exponents.

☐

Example 2

Simplify each expression. Write your answer in exponential form.

A. $\dfrac{7^5}{7^3}$

☐ ☐ exponents.

☐

B. $\dfrac{x^{10}}{x^9}$

☐ Subtract ☐.

☐ Think: $x^1 = $ ☐

Holt Mathematics

Example 3

Simplify each expression. Write your answer in exponential form.

A. $(5^4)^2$

exponents.

B. $(6^7)^9$

exponents.

C. $\left(\left(\frac{2}{3}\right)^{12}\right)^{-3}$

exponents.

D. $(17^2)^{-20}$

exponents.

Check It Out!

1. Simplify. Write your answer in exponential form.

$4^2 \cdot 4^4$

2. Simplify. Write your answer in exponential form.

$\dfrac{9^9}{9^2}$

3. Simplify. Write your answer in exponential form.

$(3^3)^4$

Holt Mathematics

LESSON 4-4 Multiplying and Dividing Monomials

Lesson Objectives

Multiply and divide polynomials and take powers of monomials.

Vocabulary

monomial (p. 180) _____

_____

Additional Examples

Example 1

Multiply.

A. $(3a^2)(4a^5)$

$(3 \cdot 4)(a^2 \cdot a^5)$ Use the ☐ Properties.

$3 \cdot 4 \cdot a^{\boxed{}}$

☐   coefficients.
          exponents that have the same base.

B. $(4x^2y^3)(5xy^5)$

$(4 \cdot 5)(x^2 \cdot x)(y^3 \cdot y^5)$ Use the ☐ Properties.

$(4 \cdot 5)(x^2 \cdot x^{\boxed{}})(y^3 \cdot y^5)$ Think: $x = \boxed{}$.

$4 \cdot 5 \cdot x^{\boxed{}} \cdot y^{\boxed{}}$ Multiply ☐.

☐   Add ☐ that have the same base.

C. $(-3p^2r)\,(6pr^3s)$ Use the ☐ Properties.

$(-3 \cdot 6)(p^2 \cdot p)(r \cdot r^3)(s)$

$(-3 \cdot 6)(p^2 \cdot p^{\boxed{}})(r^{\boxed{}} \cdot r^3)(s)$ Think: $p = \boxed{}$; $r = \boxed{}$

$(-3) \cdot 6 \cdot p^{\boxed{}} \cdot r^{\boxed{}} \cdot s$ Multiply coefficients. Add exponents that

☐   have the same ☐.

Holt Mathematics

Example 2

Divide. Assume that no denominator equals zero.

$$\frac{18a^2b^3}{16ab^3}$$

$$\frac{18}{16}a^{\boxed{}} \cdot b^{\boxed{}}$$ Divide $\boxed{}$.

$$\frac{9}{8}a^{\boxed{}} \, b^{\boxed{}}$$ Subtract $\boxed{}$ that have the same base.

$\boxed{}$ Think: $b^0 = \boxed{}$

Example 3

Simplify.

A. $(3y)^3$

$$3^{\boxed{}} \cdot y^{\boxed{}}$$ Raise each factor to the $\boxed{}$.

$\boxed{}$

B. $(2a^2b^6)^4$

$$2^{\boxed{}} \cdot (a^{\boxed{}})^{\boxed{}} \cdot (b^{\boxed{}})^{\boxed{}}$$ Raise each factor to the $\boxed{}$.

$$2^{\boxed{}} \cdot a^{\boxed{}} \cdot b^{\boxed{}}$$ Multiply $\boxed{}$.

$\boxed{}$

Check It Out!

1. Multiply.

$$(4n^4) \cdot (5n^3)(p)$$ $\boxed{}$

2. Divide. Assume that no denominator equals zero.

$$\frac{12m^2n^3}{9mn^2}$$ $\boxed{}$

3. Simplify.

$$(4a)^4$$ $\boxed{}$

Holt Mathematics

Scientific Notation

LESSON 4-5

Lesson Objectives

Express large and small numbers in scientific notation and compare two numbers written in scientific notation

Vocabulary

scientific notation (p. 184) _____

_____

Additional Examples

Example 1

Multiply.

14×10^4

14.0000   Since the exponent is a positive ☐,

[   ]   move the decimal point ☐ places to the right.

Example 2

Write the number in scientific notation.

0.00709   Think: The decimal point needs to move ☐ places to get to a number between 1 and 10.

[   ]   Think: The number is less than 1, so the

exponent will be [   ].

Example 3

Write the number in standard form.

2.7×10^{-3}

002.7   Think: Move the decimal point [   ] 3 places.

[   ]

Holt Mathematics

Example 4

A certain cell has a diameter of approximately 4.11×10^{-5} meters. A second cell has a diameter of 1.5×10^{-5} meters. Which cell has a greater diameter?

4.11×10^{-5} Compare the [＿＿＿＿].
   1.5×10^{-5}

4.11 [＿] 1.5 Compare the values between [＿＿＿＿].

                    4.11×10^{-5} [＿] 1.5×10^{-5}.

The first cell has a [＿＿＿＿] diameter.

Check It Out!

1. Multiply.

     2.5×10^5

2. Write the number in scientific notation.

     0.000811

3. Write the number in standard form.

     1.9×10^{-5}

4. A star has a diameter of approximately 5.11×10^3 kilometers. A second star has a diameter of 5×10^4 kilometers. Which star has a greater diameter?

Holt Mathematics

LESSON 4-6 **Squares and Square Roots**

Lesson Objectives

Find square roots of numbers and monomials

Vocabulary

perfect square (p. 192) _____

_____

square root (p. 192) _____

_____

principal square root (p. 192) _____

_____

Additional Examples

Example 1

Find the two square roots of each number.

A. 49

$\sqrt{49}$ = [ ]   [ ] is a square root, since $7 \cdot 7 =$ [ ].

$-\sqrt{49}$ = [ ]   [ ] is also a square root, since $-7 \cdot (-7) =$ [ ].

The square roots of 49 are [ ]

B. 100

$\sqrt{100}$ = [ ]   [ ] is a square root, since $10 \cdot 10 =$ [ ].

$-\sqrt{100}$ = [ ]   [ ] is also a square root, since $-10 \cdot (-10) =$

[ ]. The square roots of 100 are [ ]

Holt Mathematics

Example 2

A square window has an area of 169 square inches. How wide is the window?

Find the square root of [   ] to find the width of the window. Use the

[   ] square root; a negative length has no meaning.

[   ] $= 169$

So $\sqrt{169} = $ [   ].

The window is [   ] inches wide.

Example 3

Simplify each expression.

A. $\sqrt{144c^2}$

$\sqrt{144c^2} = \sqrt{()^2}$ Write the monomial as a [   ].

$= $ [   ] Use the [   ] symbol.

B. $\sqrt{z^6}$

$\sqrt{z^6} = \sqrt{(z^{})^{}}$ Write the monomial as a [   ]:

$z^6 = (z^{})^{}$

$= $ [   ] Use the [   ] symbol.

C. $\sqrt{100n^4}$

$\sqrt{100n^4} = \sqrt{()^{}}$ Write the monomial as a [   ].

$= $ [   ] $10n^2$ is [   ] for all values of n.

The [   ] symbol is not needed.

Holt Mathematics

Check It Out!

1. Find the two square roots of the number.

144

2. A square-shaped kitchen table has an area of 16 square feet. Will it fit through a van door that has a 5-foot wide opening?

3. Simplify.

$\sqrt{121r^2}$

Holt Mathematics

LESSON 4-7 Estimating Square Roots

Lesson Objectives

Estimate square roots of numbers

Additional Examples

Example 1

Name the two integers that $\sqrt{55}$ is in between. Explain your answer.

$\sqrt{55}$

[ ] , [ ] , [ ] , [ ]   List [ ] squares near 55.

[ ] < 55 < [ ]   Find the perfect squares nearest 55.

$\sqrt{\boxed{}}$ < $\sqrt{55}$ < $\sqrt{\boxed{}}$ Find the [ ] of the perfect squares.

[ ] < $\sqrt{55}$ < [ ]

$\sqrt{55}$ is between [ ] and [ ] because 55 is between [ ] and [ ].

Example 2

A Coast Guard boat searching for a lost sailboat covers a square area of 185 mi². What is the approximate length of each side of the square area? Round your answer to the nearest mile.

[ ] , [ ] , [ ] , [ ]   List perfect squares near 185.

[ ] < 185 < [ ]   Find the perfect squares nearest 185.

$\sqrt{\boxed{}}$ < $\sqrt{185}$ < $\sqrt{\boxed{}}$ Find the [ ] of the perfect squares. 185 is closer to 196 than 169, so $\sqrt{185}$ is closer to

[ ] < $\sqrt{185}$ < [ ]

$\sqrt{185} \approx$ [ ]   [ ] than [ ]. Each side of the search area is about [ ] miles long.

91
Holt Mathematics

Example 3

Approximate $\sqrt{135}$ to the nearest hundredth.

Step 1: Find the value of the whole number.

$\boxed{} < 135 < \boxed{}$ Find the $\underline{}$ squares nearest 135.

$\sqrt{\boxed{}} < \sqrt{135} < \sqrt{\boxed{}}$ Find the $\underline{}$ of the perfect squares.

$\boxed{} < \sqrt{135} < \boxed{}$ The number will be between $\boxed{}$ and $\boxed{}$.

The whole number part of the answer is $\boxed{}$.

Step 2: Find the value of the decimal.

$135 - 121 = \boxed{}$ Find the $\underline{}$ between the given number, 135, and the lower perfect square.

$144 - 121 = \boxed{}$ Find the $\underline{}$ between the greater perfect square and the lower perfect square.

$\dfrac{14}{23}$ Write the difference as a ratio.

$14 \div 23 \approx \boxed{}$ Divide to find the approximate decimal value.

Step 3: Find the approximate value.

$\boxed{} + \boxed{} = \boxed{}$ Combine the whole number and decimal.

$\boxed{} \approx \boxed{}$ Round to the nearest hundredth.

The approximate value of $\sqrt{135}$ to the nearest hundredth is $\boxed{}$.

Holt Mathematics

Example 4

Use a calculator to find $\sqrt{600}$. Round to the nearest tenth.

$\sqrt{600} \approx$ [   ] Use a calculator.

$\sqrt{600} \approx$ [   ] Round to the nearest tenth.

$\sqrt{600}$ rounded to the nearest tenth is [   ].

Check It Out!

The square root is between two integers. Name the integers.

1. $\sqrt{80}$

2. A tent was advertised in the newspaper as having an enclosed square area of 168 ft². What is the approximate length of the sides of the square area? Round your answer to the nearest foot.

3. Approximate $\sqrt{180}$ to the nearest hundredth.

4. Use a calculator to find $\sqrt{800}$. Round to the nearest tenth.

Holt Mathematics

LESSON 4-8

The Real Numbers

Lesson Objectives

Determine if a number is rational or irrational

Vocabulary

real number (p. 200) _____

_____

irrational number (p. 200) _____

_____

Density Property (p. 201) _____

_____

Additional Examples

Example 1

Write all classifications that apply to each number.

A. $\sqrt{5}$ 5 is a [____] number that is not a perfect [____].

B. -12.75 -12.75 is a [_____] decimal.

C. $\dfrac{\sqrt{16}}{2}$ $\dfrac{\sqrt{16}}{2} = \dfrac{4}{2} = 2$

Holt Mathematics

Example 2

State if each number is rational, irrational, or not a real number.

A. $\sqrt{21}$

B. $\frac{0}{3}$ $\frac{0}{3} = \boxed{}$

C. $\frac{4}{0}$

Example 3

Find a real number between $3\frac{2}{5}$ and $3\frac{3}{5}$.

There are many solutions. One solution is halfway between the two numbers. To find it, add the numbers and divide by 2.

$$\left(3\frac{2}{5} + 3\frac{3}{5}\right) \div 2 = \boxed{}\frac{\boxed{}}{5} \div 2 = \boxed{} \div 2 = \boxed{}.$$

A real number between $3\frac{2}{5}$ and $3\frac{3}{5}$ is $\boxed{}$.

Check: Use a graph.

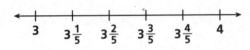

Check It Out!

1. Write all names that apply to the number.

$\sqrt{9}$

2. State if the number is rational, irrational, or not a real number.

$\sqrt{23}$

3. Find a real number between $4\frac{3}{7}$ and $4\frac{4}{7}$.

Holt Mathematics

California Standards ⬤━MG3.3

LESSON 4-9 The Pythagorean Theorem

Lesson Objectives

Use the Pythagorean Theorem and its corollaries to solve problems

Vocabulary

Pythagorean Theorem (p. 205) _____

_____

leg (p. 205) _____

_____

hypotenuse (p. 205) _____

_____

Additional Examples

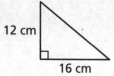

Use the Pythagorean Theorem to find each missing measure.

A.

12 cm, 16 cm (right triangle)

$$a^2 + b^2 = c^2 \qquad \text{Use the } \boxed{} \text{ Theorem.}$$

$$\boxed{}^2 + \boxed{}^2 = c^2 \qquad \text{Substitute for } a \text{ and } b.$$

$$\boxed{} + \boxed{} = c^2 \qquad \text{Evaluate the powers.}$$

$$\boxed{} = c^2 \qquad \text{Add.}$$

$$\boxed{} = \sqrt{c^2} \qquad \text{Take the square root of both sides.}$$

$$\boxed{} = c \qquad \text{The length of the hypotenuse is } \boxed{}.$$

Holt Mathematics

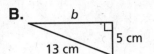

LESSON 4-9 *CONTINUED*

Use the Pythagorean Theorem to find each missing measure.

B.

A right triangle with hypotenuse 13 cm, one leg 5 cm, and the top leg labeled b.

$a^2 + b^2 = c^2$ Use the Pythagorean Theorem.

$\boxed{}^2 + b^2 = \boxed{}^2$ Substitute for a and c.

$\boxed{} + b^2 = \boxed{}$ Evaluate the powers.

$\underline{-\boxed{} \qquad\qquad -\boxed{}}$ Subtract $\boxed{}$ from both sides.

$b^2 = \boxed{}$

$\boxed{} = \boxed{}$ Take the square root of both sides.

$b = \boxed{}$ The length of the missing leg is $\boxed{}$ cm.

PROBLEM SOLVING APPLICATION

A square field has sides of 75 feet. About how far is it from one corner of the field to the opposite corner of the field? Round your answer to the nearest tenth.

1. Understand the Problem

Rewrite the question as a statement:

- Find the distance from one corner of the field to the opposite corner of the field.

List the **important information**:

- Drawing a segment from one corner of the field to the opposite corner of the field divides the field into two right triangles.

- The segment between the two corners is the hypotenuse.

- The sides of the field are legs, and they are each 75 feet long.

Holt Mathematics

2. **Make a Plan**

You can use the Pythagorean Theorem to write an equation.

3. **Solve**

$$a^2 + b^2 = c^2 \qquad \text{Use the Pythagorean Theorem.}$$

$$\boxed{}^2 + \boxed{}^2 = c^2 \qquad \text{Substitute for } a \text{ and } b.$$

$$\boxed{} + \boxed{} = c^2 \qquad \text{Evaluate the } \boxed{}.$$

$$\boxed{} = c^2 \qquad \text{Add.}$$

$$\boxed{} = c \qquad \text{Take the } \boxed{}$$
$$\text{of both sides.}$$

$$\boxed{} = c \qquad \text{Round.}$$

The distance from one corner of the field to the opposite corner is about

$$\boxed{} \text{ ft.}$$

4. **Look Back**

The hypotenuse is the longest side of a right triangle. Since the distance from one corner of the field to the opposite corner is greater than the length of a side of the field, the answer is reasonable.

Example 3

Tell whether the given side lengths form a right triangle.

A. 12, 35, 37

$$a^2 + b^2 \overset{?}{=} c^2 \qquad \text{Compare } a^2 \text{ to } b^2 \text{ to } c^2.$$

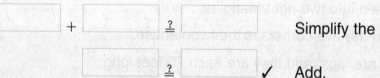

$$\boxed{}^2 + \boxed{}^2 \overset{?}{=} \boxed{}^2 \qquad \text{Substitute the longest side length for } c.$$

$$\boxed{} + \boxed{} \overset{?}{=} \boxed{} \qquad \text{Simplify the powers.}$$

$$\boxed{} \overset{?}{=} \boxed{} \checkmark \qquad \text{Add.}$$

The side lengths $\boxed{}$ a right triangle.

Holt Mathematics

Tell whether the given side lengths form a right triangle.

B. 8, 12, 16

$$a^2 + b^2 \overset{?}{=} c^2$$

Compare a^2 to b^2 to c^2.

$$\boxed{}^2 + \boxed{}^2 \overset{?}{=} \boxed{}^2$$

Substitute the longest side length for c.

$$\boxed{} + \boxed{} \overset{?}{=} \boxed{}$$

Simplify the powers.

$$\boxed{} \neq \boxed{} \quad \textbf{\textit{x}}$$

Add.

The side lengths ▨▨▨▨▨ a right triangle.

Check It Out!

1. Use the Pythagorean Theorem to find the missing measure.

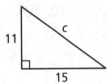

2. A rectangular field has a length of 100 yards and a width of 33 yards. About how far is it from one corner of the field to the opposite corner of the field? Round your answer to the nearest tenth.

3. Tell whether the given side lengths form a right triangle.

8, 15, 17

Holt Mathematics

4-1 Exponents

Simplify.

1. 4^3

2. 2^5

3. $(-6)^4$

4. -7^3

Write in exponential form.

5. 10

6. $9 \cdot 9 \cdot 9 \cdot q \cdot q$

7. $-26 \cdot -26 \cdot -26$

8. $5c \cdot 5c \cdot 5c \cdot 5c$

4-2 Integer Exponents

Simplify the powers of 10.

9. 10^{-4}

10. 10^0

11. 10^{-5}

12. 10^{-3}

Simplify.

13. $(-2)^{-4}$

14. -3^{-2}

15. 4^{-5}

16. $10 - 5^0 + (4 + 1)^{-2} - (2 - 1)^{-1}$

4-3 Properties of Exponents

Simplify each expression. Write your answer in exponential form.

17. $6^2 \cdot 6^5$

18. $y^{10} \cdot y^{10}$

19. $8^1 \cdot 8^0$

20. $a^4 \cdot a^{-3}$

21. $\dfrac{3^5}{3^3}$

22. $\dfrac{p^{11}}{p^6}$

23. $\dfrac{r^7}{r^{-14}}$

24. $\dfrac{c^{-5}}{c^{-2}}$

Holt Mathematics

4-4 Multiplying and Dividing Monomials

Multiply or divide. Assume that no denominator equals zero.

25. $(5f^2)(6f^3)$ **26.** $\dfrac{25c^3d^3}{5cd^2}$ **27.** $\dfrac{10g^{13}}{8g^9}$ **28.** $(-4s^3t^2)(5s^2t)$

Simplify.

29. $(2b)^5$ **30.** $(3f^2g^3)^2$ **31.** $(5b)^2$ **32.** $(6xy^4)^3$

4-5 Scientific Notation

Multiply.

33. 4.6×10^8 **34.** -2.3×10^{-3} **35.** 5.55×10^{10}

Write each number in scientific notation.

36. $7,456,000,000$ **37.** $-3,000,000,000,000,000$ **38.** 0.000000204

39. The distance from Earth to Mars is 7,839,000 km. A satellite traveled from Earth to Mars 100 times. How many km did the satellite travel? Write your answer in scientific notation.

4-6 Squares and Square Roots

Find the two square roots of each number.

40. 36   **41.** 625   **42.** 900   **43.** 289

Simplify each expression.

44. $\sqrt{49} - 10$ **45.** $\sqrt{\dfrac{64}{16}}$ **46.** $\sqrt{49} \cdot \sqrt{4}$

Holt Mathematics

4-7 Estimating Square Roots

Each square root is between two integers. Name the integers.

47. $\sqrt{5}$ **48.** $-\sqrt{43}$ **49.** $\sqrt{1{,}000}$ **50.** $\sqrt{75}$

Use a calculator to find each value. Round to the nearest tenth.

51. $\sqrt{63}$ **52.** $\sqrt{105}$ **53.** $\sqrt{28.7}$ **54.** $\sqrt{56}$

4-8 The Real Numbers

Write all classifications that apply to each number.

55. $\sqrt{81}$ **56.** $\sqrt{11}$ **57.** 3.75   **58.** -4

Find a real number between each pair of numbers.

59. $6\frac{1}{4}$ and $6\frac{1}{2}$ **60.** 2.87 and $\frac{32}{11}$ **61.** $\frac{2}{5}$ and $\frac{2}{3}$

4-9 The Pythagorean Theorem

Use the Pythagorean Theorem to find each missing measure.

62.

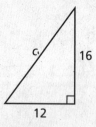

63.

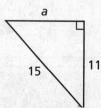

Holt Mathematics

Big Ideas

Answer these questions to summarize the important concepts from Chapter 4 in your own words.

1. Explain how to evaluate 3^6.

2. Explain the difference between 3.56×10^8 and 3.56×10^{-8}.

3. Explain why $\sqrt{81} = \pm 9$.

4. Explain $\sqrt{-25} \neq \pm 5$.

5. Explain how to estimate $\sqrt{60}$.

6. Explain why $0.\overline{3}$ is a rational number.

For more review of Chapter 4:

- Complete the Chapter 4 Study Guide and Review on pages 214–216 of your textbook.
- Complete the Ready to Go On quizzes on pages 190 and 210 of your textbook.

Holt Mathematics

Ratios

Lesson Objectives

Write and compare ratios.

Vocabulary

ratio (p. 232) _____

equivalent ratios (p. 232) _____

Additional Examples

Example 1

Write the ratio 15 bikes to 9 skateboards in simplest form.

$$\frac{\text{bikes}}{\text{skateboards}} = \frac{15}{9}$$ Write the ratio as a fraction.

$$= \frac{15 \div \boxed{}}{9 \div} = \boxed{}$$ Simplify.

The ratio of bikes to skateboards is ▭.

Example 2

Write the ratio 3 yards to 12 feet in simplest form.

First convert yards to feet.

3 yards = 3 · 3 feet   There are 3 feet in each yard.

$\qquad\quad$ = 9 feet   Multiply.

Now write the ratio.

$$\frac{3 \text{ yards}}{12 \text{ feet}} = \frac{9 \text{ feet}}{12 \text{ feet}} = \frac{9 \div \boxed{}}{12 \div} = \boxed{}$$ Simplify.

The ratio is ▭.

Holt Mathematics

Example 3

Simplify to tell whether the ratios are equivalent.

A. $\frac{3}{27}$ and $\frac{2}{18}$ $\frac{3}{27} = \frac{3 \div \boxed{}}{27 \div \boxed{}} = \boxed{}$

Since $\boxed{} = \boxed{}$, the ratios are

$\frac{2}{18} = \frac{2 \div \boxed{}}{18 \div \boxed{}} = \boxed{}$

$\boxed{}$.

B. $\frac{12}{15}$ and $\frac{27}{36}$ $\frac{12}{15} = \frac{12 \div \boxed{}}{15 \div \boxed{}} = \boxed{}$

Since $\boxed{} \ne \boxed{}$, the ratios are

$\frac{27}{36} = \frac{27 \div \boxed{}}{36 \div \boxed{}} = \boxed{}$

$\boxed{}$.

Example 4

At 4°C, four cubic feet of silver has the same mass as 42 cubic feet of water. At 4°C, would 20 cubic feet of silver have the same mass as 210 cubic feet of water?

$\frac{4}{42} \overset{?}{=} \frac{20}{210} \leftarrow \text{ft}^3 \text{ silver} \\ \phantom{\frac{4}{42} \overset{?}{=} \frac{20}{210}} \leftarrow \text{ft}^3 \text{ water}$

$\frac{4 \div \boxed{}}{42 \div \boxed{}} \overset{?}{=} \frac{20 \div \boxed{}}{210 \div \boxed{}}$ Divide.

$\boxed{} = \boxed{}$.   Simplify.

Since $\boxed{} = \boxed{}$, 210 cubic feet of water would have

$\boxed{}$ mass at 4°C as 20 cubic feet of silver.

Holt Mathematics

Check It Out!

1. Write the ratio 24 shirts to 9 jeans in simplest form.

2. Write the ratio 36 inches to 4 feet in simplest form.

3. Simplify to tell whether the ratios are equivalent.

   $\frac{14}{49}$ and $\frac{16}{36}$

4. At 4°C, two cubic feet of silver has the same mass as 21 cubic feet of water. At 4°C, would 105 cubic feet of water have the same mass as 10 cubic feet of silver?

Holt Mathematics

Rates and Unit Rates

Lesson Objectives

Work with rates and unit rates

Additional Examples

Example 1

Geoff can type 30 words in half a minute. How many words can he type in 1 minute?

$$\frac{\boxed{} \text{ words}}{\boxed{} \text{ minute}}$$

Write the rate.

$$\frac{\boxed{} \text{ words} \cdot 2}{\boxed{} \text{ minute} \cdot 2} = \frac{\boxed{} \text{ words}}{\boxed{} \text{ minute}}$$

Multiply to find words per minute.

Geoff can type $\boxed{}$ words in one minute.

Example 2

Five cubic meters of copper has a mass of 44,800 kilograms. What is the density of copper?

$$\frac{\boxed{} \text{ kg}}{\boxed{} \text{ m}^3}$$

Write the rate.

$$\frac{\boxed{} \div 5\text{kg}}{\boxed{} \div 5\text{m}^3}$$

Divide to find kilograms per 1 m^3.

$$\frac{\boxed{} \text{ kg}}{\boxed{} \text{ m}^3}$$

Copper has a density of $\boxed{}$ kg/m^3.

Holt Mathematics

Example 3

Estimate each unit rate.

A. 468 students to 91 computers

$$\frac{468 \text{ students}}{91 \text{ computers}} \approx \frac{\boxed{} \text{ students}}{\boxed{} \text{ computers}}$$ Choose a number close to 468 that is divisible by 91.

$$\approx \frac{\boxed{} \text{ students}}{\boxed{} \text{ computer}}$$ Divide to find students per computer.

468 students to 91 computers is approximately $\boxed{}$ students per computer.

B. 313 feet in 8 seconds

$$\frac{313 \text{ feet}}{8 \text{ seconds}} \approx \frac{\boxed{} \text{ feet}}{\boxed{} \text{ seconds}}$$ Choose a number close to 313 that is divisible by 8.

$$\approx \frac{\boxed{} \text{ feet}}{\boxed{} \text{ second}}$$ Divide to find feet per second.

313 feet in 8 seconds is approximately $\boxed{}$ feet per second.

Example 4

A. Pens can be purchased in a 5-pack for $1.95 or a 15-pack for $6.20. Which pack has the lower unit price?

$$\frac{\text{price for package}}{\text{number of pens}} = \frac{\$\boxed{}}{\boxed{} \text{ pens}} = \boxed{} \text{ per pen}$$ Divide the price by the number of pens.

$$\frac{\text{price for package}}{\text{number of pens}} = \frac{\$\boxed{}}{\boxed{} \text{ pens}} \approx \boxed{} \text{ per pen}$$

The $\boxed{}$-pack for $\boxed{}$ has the lower unit price.

Holt Mathematics

B. Jamie can buy a 15 oz jar of peanut butter for $2.19 or a 20 oz jar for $2.78. Which jar has the lower unit price?

$\dfrac{\text{price for jar}}{\text{number of ounces}}$ = [   ] ≈ [   ]   Divide the price by the number of ounces.

$\dfrac{\text{price for jar}}{\text{number of ounces}}$ = [   ] ≈ [   ]   Divide the price by the number of ounces.

The [   ] oz jar for [   ] has the lower unit price.

Check It Out!

1. Penelope can type 90 words in 2 minutes. How many words can she type in 1 minute?

2. Four cubic meters of precious metal has a mass of 18,128 kilograms. What is the density of the precious metal?

3. Estimate the unit rate.

   583 soccer players to 85 soccer balls

4. Golf balls can be purchased in a 3-pack for $4.95 or a 12-pack for $18.95. Which pack has the lower price?

Holt Mathematics

Proportions

Lesson Objectives

Solve proportions

Vocabulary

proportion (p. 232) _____

_____

cross products (p. 232) _____

_____

Additional Examples

Example 1

Tell whether the ratios are proportional.

A. $\frac{6}{15} \overset{?}{=} \frac{4}{10}$

$\frac{6}{15} \overset{?}{\times} \frac{4}{10}$ Find the [ ] products.

$6 \cdot 10 \overset{?}{=} 4 \cdot 15$

[ ] = [ ]

Since the cross products are [ ], the ratios [ ] proportional.

B. A mixture of fuel for a certain small engine should be 4 parts gasoline to 1 part oil. If you combine 5 quarts of oil with 15 quarts of gasoline, will the mixture be correct?

$\frac{4 \text{ parts gasoline}}{1 \text{ part oil}} \overset{?}{=} \frac{15 \text{ quarts gasoline}}{5 \text{ quarts oil}}$ Set up equal ratios.

$\frac{4}{1} \overset{?}{\times} \frac{15}{5}$ Find the cross [ ].

[ ] · [ ] = 20   [ ] · [ ] = [ ]

[ ] ≠ [ ]

The ratios [ ] equal. The mixture [ ] correct.

Holt Mathematics

Example 2

The ratio of the length of the actual height of a person to the length of the shadow cast by the person is 1:3. At the same time, a lighthouse casts a shadow that is 36 meters long. What should the length of its shadow be?

$\dfrac{\text{height of person}}{\text{length of shadow}} \rightarrow \dfrac{1}{3}$ Write a ratio comparing the height of a person to shadow length.

$\dfrac{1}{3} = \dfrac{x}{36}$ Set up the proportion.
Let x represent the shadow length.

$\boxed{}\ \dfrac{1}{3} = \boxed{}\ \dfrac{x}{36}$ Since x is divided by 36, multiply both sides of the equation by $\boxed{}$.

$\boxed{} = x$ The length of the lighthouse's shadow should be $\boxed{}$ meters.

Example 3

Allyson weighs 55 lbs and sits on a seesaw 4 ft away from its center. If Marco sits 5 ft away from the center and the seesaw is balanced, how much does Marco weigh?

$\dfrac{\text{weight 1}}{\text{length 2}} = \dfrac{\text{weight 2}}{\text{length 1}}$ Set up a $\boxed{}$ using the information.

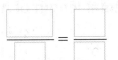 Let x represent Marco's weight.

 Find the cross products.

$\boxed{} = \boxed{}\ x$ Multiply.

$\dfrac{220}{\boxed{}} = \dfrac{5x}{\boxed{}}$ Divide both sides by $\boxed{}$.

$\boxed{} = x$ Simplify.

Marco weighs lb.

Example 4

Nate has 225 envelopes to prepare for mailing. He takes 30 minutes to prepare 45 envelopes. If he continues at the same rate, how many more minutes until he has completed the job?

Let x represent the number of minutes it takes to complete the job.

$\dfrac{30}{45} = \dfrac{x}{225}$ Set up the proportion.

$30 \cdot 225 = 45x$ Find the cross [ ].

$\dfrac{6750}{\boxed{}} = \dfrac{45x}{\boxed{}}$ Divide both sides by $\boxed{}$.

$\boxed{} = x$ Simplify.

Nate has already spent 30 minutes, so it will take him $\boxed{} - 30 = \boxed{}$ more minutes to finish the job.

Check It Out!

1. Tell whether the ratios are proportional.

   $\dfrac{5}{10} \overset{?}{=} \dfrac{2}{4}$

2. For most cats, the ratio of the length of its head to its total body length is 1:5. If a cat is 20 inches in length, what should the total length of its head be?

3. Austin weighs 32 pounds and sits on a seesaw 6 feet away from its center. If Kaylee sits on the seesaw 4 feet away from the center and the seesaw is balanced, how much does Kaylee weigh?

4. Nemo has to make 160 muffins for the bake sale. He takes 21 minutes to make 24 muffins. If he continues at the same rate, how many more minutes until he has completed the job?

Holt Mathematics

California Standards MG1.1

LESSON 5-4 Dimensional Analysis

Lesson Objectives

Use one or more conversion factors to solve rate problems

Vocabulary

conversion factor (p. 237) _____

_____

_____

Additional Examples

Example 1

The average American uses 580 pounds of paper per year. Find this rate in pounds per month, to the nearest tenth.

Convert the rate 580 pounds per year to pounds per month.

$$\frac{580 \text{ lb}}{1 \text{ yr}} \cdot \frac{1 \text{ yr}}{12 \text{ mo}}$$

To convert the second amount in a rate, multiply by the

[_____] factor with that unit in the first quantity.

$$= \frac{[\quad] \text{ lb}}{[\quad] \text{ mo}}$$

Divide out like units. $\frac{\text{lb}}{\cancel{\text{yr}}} \cdot \frac{\cancel{\text{yr}}}{\text{mo}} = \frac{\text{lb}}{\text{mo}}$

$$= [\quad] \text{ lb per month}$$

Divide 580 by 12.

The average American uses [____] pounds of paper per month.

Holt Mathematics

Example 2

PROBLEM SOLVING APPLICATION

A car traveled 60 miles on a road in 2 hours. Find this rate in feet per second.

1. **Understand the Problem**

   The problem is stated in units of miles and hours. The question asks for the answer in units of feet and seconds. You will need to use conversion factors. List the important information:

   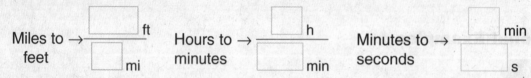

   Miles to → $\dfrac{\boxed{}\text{ ft}}{\boxed{}\text{ mi}}$ Hours to → $\dfrac{\boxed{}\text{ h}}{\boxed{}\text{ min}}$ Minutes to → $\dfrac{\boxed{}\text{ min}}{\boxed{}\text{ s}}$

   feet   minutes   seconds

2. **Make a Plan**

   You know the conversion factor that converts miles to feet. So multiply by each conversion factor separately, or simplify the problem and multiply by several conversion factors at once.

3. **Solve**

   $$\dfrac{60 \text{ mi}}{2 \text{ h}} = \dfrac{(60 \div 2)\text{ mi}}{(2 \div 2)\text{ h}} = \dfrac{\boxed{}\text{ mi}}{\boxed{}\text{ h}}$$ Convert to miles per hour.

   Create a single conversion factor to convert hours directly to seconds:

   hours to minutes → $\dfrac{\boxed{}\text{ h}}{\boxed{}\text{ min}}$; minutes to seconds → $\dfrac{\boxed{}\text{ min}}{\boxed{}\text{ s}}$

   hours to seconds $= \dfrac{1 \text{ h}}{60 \text{ min}} \cdot \dfrac{1 \text{ min}}{60 \text{ s}} = \dfrac{1\text{h}}{3600\text{s}}$

   $\dfrac{30 \text{ mi}}{1\text{h}} \cdot \dfrac{5280 \text{ ft}}{1 \text{ mi}} \cdot \dfrac{1 \text{ h}}{3600 \text{ s}}$ Set up the $\boxed{}$ factors.

   $\dfrac{30 \text{ m\!\!\!/i}}{1\text{h\!\!\!/}} \cdot \dfrac{5280 \text{ ft}}{1 \text{ m\!\!\!/i}} \cdot \dfrac{1 \text{ h\!\!\!/}}{3600 \text{ s}}$ · Divide out like units.

   $\dfrac{30 \cdot 5280 \text{ ft} \cdot 1}{1 \cdot 1 \cdot 3600 \text{ s}} = \dfrac{158{,}400 \text{ ft}}{\cdot\ 3600 \text{ s}} = \dfrac{\boxed{}\text{ ft}}{\boxed{}\text{ s}}$

Holt Mathematics

The car was traveling ☐ feet per second.

4. Look Back

A rate of ☐ ft/s is less than 50 ft/s. A rate of 60 miles in 2 hours is 30 mi/h or 0.5 mi/min.

Since 0.5 mi/min is less than 3000 ft/60 s or 50 ft/s and 44 ft/s is less than 50 ft/s, then 44 ft/s is a reasonable answer.

Example 3

A strobe lamp can be used to measure the speed of an object. The lamp flashes every $\frac{1}{100}$ of a second. A camera records the object moving 52 cm between flashes. How fast is the object moving in m/s? Use dimensional analysis to check the reasonableness of your answer.

$$\frac{52 \text{ cm}}{\frac{1}{100} \text{ s}}$$

Use rate =

$$\frac{52 \text{ cm}}{\frac{1}{100} \text{ s}} = \frac{100 \cdot 52 \text{ cm}}{100 \cdot \frac{1}{100} \text{ s}}$$

It may help to eliminate the fraction $\frac{1}{100}$ first. Multiply numerator and denominator by 100.

$$= \frac{\boxed{} \text{ cm}}{\boxed{} \text{ s}}$$

Convert centimeters to ☐ to see if the answer is reasonable.

$$\frac{\boxed{} \text{ cm}}{\boxed{} \text{ s}} \cdot \frac{1 \text{ m}}{\boxed{} \text{ cm}}$$

Multiply by the conversion factor.

$$= \frac{\boxed{} \text{ m}}{\boxed{} \text{ s}} = \frac{52 \text{ m}}{1 \text{ s}}$$

The object is traveling ☐ m/s.

Holt Mathematics

Check It Out!

1. Sam drives his car 23,040 miles per year. Find the number of miles driven per month, to the nearest mile.

2. A train traveled 180 miles on a railroad track in 4 hours. Find this rate in feet per second.

3. A strobe lamp can be used to measure the speed of an object. The lamp flashes every $\frac{1}{100}$ of a second. A camera records the object moving 65 cm between flashes. How fast is the object moving in m/s?

Holt Mathematics

LESSON 5-5 **Similar Figures**

Lesson Objectives

Determine whether figures are similar and find missing dimensions in similar figures

Vocabulary

similar (p. 244) _____

corresponding sides (p. 244) _____

_____

corresponding angles (p. 244) _____

_____

Additional Examples

Example 1

Which rectangles are similar?

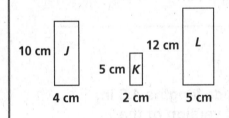

Since the three figures are all rectangles, all the angles are [　　　　] angles. So the corresponding angles are congruent.

Compare the ratios of corresponding [　　　　] to see if they are equal.

$$\frac{\text{length of rectangle } J}{\text{length of rectangle } K} \rightarrow \frac{10}{5} \overset{?}{=} \frac{4}{2} \leftarrow \frac{\text{width of rectangle } J}{\text{width of rectangle } K}$$

[　　　] = [　　　]

The ratios are [　　　　]. Rectangle J is [　　　　] to rectangle K.

The notation J [　　] K shows similarity.

$$\frac{\text{length of rectangle } J}{\text{length of rectangle } L} \rightarrow \frac{10}{12} \overset{?}{=} \frac{4}{5} \leftarrow \frac{\text{width of rectangle } J}{\text{width of rectangle } L}$$

[　　　] ≠ [　　　]

The ratios are [　　　　] equal. Rectangle J is [　　　] similar to rectangle L.

Therefore, rectangle K is [　　　] similar to rectangle L.

Holt Mathematics

LESSON 5-5 *CONTINUED*

Example 2

A picture 10 in. tall and 14 in. wide is to be scaled to 1.5 in. tall to be displayed on a Web page. How wide should the picture be on the Web page for the two pictures to be similar?

Set up a proportion. Let *w* be the width of the picture on the Web page.

$$\frac{\text{width of a picture}}{\text{width on Web page}} \rightarrow \frac{14}{w} = \frac{10}{1.5} \leftarrow \frac{\text{height of picture}}{\text{height on Web page}}$$

$14 \cdot 1.5 = w \cdot 10$ Find the ☐ products.

☐ = ☐

☐ = ☐   Divide both sides by ☐ .

☐ = *w*

The picture on the Web page should be ☐ in. wide.

Example 3

A T-shirt design includes an isosceles triangle with side lengths 4.5 in, 4.5 in, and 6 in. An advertisement shows an enlarged version of the triangle with two sides that are each 3 ft. long. What is the length of the third side of the triangle in the advertisement?

$$\frac{\text{Side of small triangle}}{\text{Base of small triangle}} = \frac{\text{Side of large triangle}}{\text{Base of large triangle}}$$

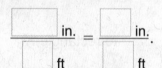

Set up a proportion.

$4.5 \cdot x = 3 \cdot 6$ Find the ☐ products.

$4.5x = 18$ Multiply.

$x = $ ☐ = ☐   Solve for *x*.

The third side of the triangle is ☐ ft long.

Holt Mathematics

Check It Out!

1. Which rectangles are similar?

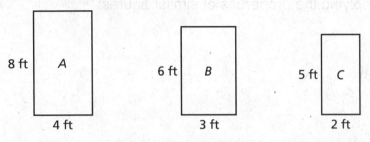

8 ft A

4 ft

6 ft B

3 ft

5 ft C

2 ft

2. A painting 40 in. tall and 56 in. wide is to be scaled to 10 in. tall to be displayed on a poster. How wide should the painting be on the poster for the two pictures to be similar?

3. A flag in the shape of an isosceles triangle with side lengths 18 ft, 18 ft, and 24 ft is hanging on a pole outside a campground. A camp t-shirt shows a smaller version of the triangle with two sides that are each 4 in. long. What is the length of the third side of the triangle on the t-shirt?

Holt Mathematics

 **California Standards** MG1.2

LESSON 5-6 **Indirect Measurement** *Know it!* *Note*

Lesson Objectives

Find measures indirectly by applying the properties of similar figures

Vocabulary

indirect measurement (p. 248) _____

_____

Additional Examples

Example 1

Triangles *ABC* and *EFG* are similar. Find the length of side *EG*.

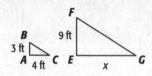

Triangles [ ] and [ ] are similar.

$\dfrac{AB}{AC} = \dfrac{EF}{EG}$ Set up a proportion.

$\dfrac{\boxed{}}{\boxed{}} = \dfrac{\boxed{}}{\boxed{}}$ Substitute [ ] for *AB*, [ ] for *AC*, and [ ] for *EF*.

$\boxed{} = \boxed{}$ Find the [   ].

$\dfrac{3x}{\boxed{}} = \dfrac{36}{\boxed{}}$ Divide both sides by $\boxed{}$.

$x = \boxed{}$

The length of side *EG* is [   ] ft.

Holt Mathematics

Example 2

PROBLEM SOLVING APPLICATION

A 30-ft building casts a shadow that is 75 ft long. A nearby tree casts a shadow that is 35 ft long. How tall is the tree?

1. Understand the Problem

The **answer** is the [   ] of the tree.
List the important information:

• The length of the building's shadow is [   ] ft.

• The height of the building is [   ] ft.

• The length of the tree's shadow is [   ] ft.

2. Make a Plan

Use the information to [   ].

3. Solve

Draw dashed lines to form triangles. The building with its shadow and the

tree with its shadow form similar [   ] triangles.

$$\frac{\boxed{}}{\boxed{}} = \frac{h}{\boxed{}}$$

Corresponding sides of similar figures are [   ].

$$\boxed{} = \boxed{}$$

Find the [   ].

$$\frac{75h}{\boxed{}} = \frac{1050}{\boxed{}}$$

Divide both sides by [   ].

$$h = \boxed{}$$

Holt Mathematics

The height of the tree is [ ] ft.

4. Look Back

Since $\dfrac{\boxed{}}{\boxed{}}$ = 2.5, the building's shadow is 2.5 times its height. So, the

tree's shadow should also be 2.5 times its height and 2.5 × [ ] is 35 feet.

Check It Out!

1. Triangles *DEF* and *GHI* are similar. Find the length of side *HI*.

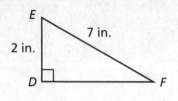
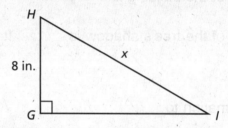

2. A 24-ft building casts a shadow that is 8 ft long. A nearby tree casts a shadow that is 3 ft long. How tall is the tree?

Holt Mathematics

LESSON 5-7 **Scale Drawing and Scale Models**

Lesson Objectives

Make comparisons between and find dimensions of scale drawings, models, and actual objects

Vocabulary

scale drawing (p. 252) _____

_____

scale model (p. 252) _____

_____

scale (p. 252) _____

_____

scale factor (p. 253) _____

_____

Additional Examples

Example 1

Under a 1000:1 microscope view, an amoeba appears to have a length of 8 mm. What is its actual length?

$$\frac{1000}{1} = \frac{\boxed{}\,\text{mm}}{x\ \text{mm}}$$ Write a proportion using the scale.
Let x be the actual length of the amoeba.

$1000 \cdot x = 1 \cdot \boxed{}$ The cross products are equal.

$x = \boxed{}$ Solve the proportion.

The actual length of the amoeba is ☐ mm.

Holt Mathematics

Example 2

The length of an object on a scale drawing is 2 cm, and its actual length is 8 m. The scale is 1 cm: ___ m. What is the scale?

$\dfrac{1\ cm}{x\ m} = \dfrac{\boxed{}\ cm}{\boxed{}\ cm}$ Set up proportion using $\dfrac{\text{scale length}}{\text{actual length}}$.

$1 \cdot \boxed{} = x \cdot \boxed{}$ Find the cross products.

$\boxed{} = 2x$

$\boxed{} = x$ Divide both sides by $\boxed{}$.

The scale is 1 cm: $\boxed{}$ m.

Example 3

A model of a 27 ft tall house was made using the scale 2 in:3 ft. What is the height of the model?

$\dfrac{2\ in.}{3\ ft} = \dfrac{2\ in.}{\boxed{}\ in.} = \dfrac{1\ in.}{18\ in.} = \boxed{}$ First find the $\boxed{}$ factor.

The scale factor for the model is $\boxed{}$. Now set up a proportion.

$\dfrac{1}{18} = \dfrac{h\ in.}{324\ in.}$ Convert: 27 ft = $\boxed{}$ in.

$\boxed{} = 18h$ Find the cross products.

$\boxed{} = h$ Divide both sides by $\boxed{}$.

The height of the model is $\boxed{}$ in.

Holt Mathematics

Example 4

A DNA model was built using the scale 5 cm:0.0000001 mm. If the model of the DNA chain is 20 cm long, what is the length of the actual chain?

$$\frac{5 \text{ cm}}{0.0000001 \text{ mm}} = \frac{50 \text{ mm}}{0.0000001 \text{ mm}} = 500{,}000{,}000 \qquad \text{Find the scale factor.}$$

The scale factor for the model is 500,000,000. This means the model is 500 million times larger than the actual chain.

$$\frac{500{,}000{,}000}{1} = \frac{20 \text{ cm}}{x \text{ cm}} \qquad \text{Set up a proportion.}$$

$$\boxed{} \qquad x = \boxed{} \cdot \boxed{} \qquad \text{Find the cross products.}$$

$$x = \boxed{} \qquad \text{Divide both sides by}$$

$$\boxed{}.$$

The length of the DNA chain is _____ cm.

Check It Out!

1. Under a 10,000:1 microscope view, a fiber appears to have a length of 1 mm. What is its actual length?

2. The length of an object on a scale drawing is 4 cm, and its actual length is 12 m. The scale is 1 cm: ___ m. What is the scale?

3. A model of a 24 ft tall bridge was made using the scale 4 in:2 ft. What is the height of the model?

4. A model was built using the scale 2 cm:0.01 mm. If the model is 30 cm long, what is the length of the actual object? Find the scale factor.

5-1 Ratios

Write each ratio in simplest form.

1. 20 apples to 4 oranges

2. 4 yards to 64 inches

Simplify to tell whether the ratios are equivalent.

3. $\frac{3}{4}$ and $\frac{21}{29}$

4. $\frac{5}{13}$ and $\frac{2.5}{6.5}$

5. $\frac{33}{81}$ and $\frac{22}{54}$

6. Tony's gas tank holds 18 gallons of gas. His gas tank has 8 gallons of gas in it. Is this equivalent to $\frac{5}{9}$ of the gas tank? If not, what amount of gas is equivalent to $\frac{5}{9}$ of the gas tank? Explain.

5-2 Rates and Unit Rates

7. Jeff runs at a rate of 6 miles/hour. How far can he run in $1\frac{1}{2}$ hours?

8. The mass of 2 cm³ of gold is 38.6 grams. Find the density of the gold.

Estimate the unit rate.

9. $3\frac{1}{2}$ sticks of butter for 3 dozen cookies

10. 95 students in 4 classes

Find the unit price for each offer and tell which has the lower unit price.

11. 8 oz. can of sauce for $1.09

48 oz. can for sauce for $4.99

12. 6 bagels for $4.25

1 dozen bagels for $7.99

Holt Mathematics

5-3 Solving Proportions

Tell whether the ratios are proportional.

13. $\frac{9}{27} \overset{?}{=} \frac{8}{24}$

14. $\frac{5}{30} \overset{?}{=} \frac{3}{16}$

15. $\frac{8}{14} \overset{?}{=} \frac{9}{16}$

16. $\frac{8}{10} \overset{?}{=} \frac{16}{20}$

17. Christopher has to wash 280 dishes. It takes him 20 minutes to wash 35 dishes. If he continues at the same rate, how many more minutes until he has washed the rest of the dishes?

5-4 Dimensional Analysis

Use conversion factors to find each unit to the nearest hundredth.

18. Liza and Taylor are on a seesaw. Liza weighs 40 pounds and is 6 feet from the fulcrum. If Taylor weighs 44 pounds, how far should she sit from the fulcrum to balance the seesaw?

19. 16 pints to quarts

20. 600 lb. to tons

21. $3\frac{1}{2}$ miles to feet

22. 288 oz. to pounds

23. 18 gallons to cups

24. 12,320 yards to miles

Holt Mathematics

5-5 Similar Figures

25. Which triangles are similar?

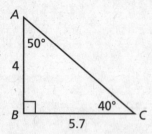 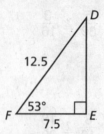 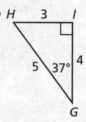

26. An isosceles triangle has a base of 15 meters and legs measuring 12 meters. How long are the legs in a similar triangle with a base of 8 meters?

5-6 Indirect Measurement

27. A house casts a shadow of 20 ft. At the same time, a 14 ft. flagpole casts a shadow of 8.75 ft. How tall is the house?

28. A 30 ft. tree casts a shadow of 12 ft. A 6 ft. 3 in. man is standing nearby. How long is his shadow?

5-7 Scale Drawings and Scale Models

29. On the blueprint of a house, the family room is a 6 in. by 4 in. rectangle. If the blueprint has a scale of 1 in. = 2.5 ft., what are the dimensions of the actual room?

30. The scale of a drawing is $\frac{1}{4}$ in.:5 ft. Find the length of a drawing with an actual length of 15 ft.

Holt Mathematics

CHAPTER
5

Answer these questions to summarize the important concepts from Chapter 5 in your own words.

1. Explain how to find two ratios equivalent to $\frac{12}{6}$.

2. Explain how to solve the proportion $\frac{40}{15} = \frac{30}{x}$ using equivalent fractions.

3. The length of an object on a scale drawing is 5 in., and its actual length is 50 ft. Explain how to find the scale.

For more review of Chapter 5:

- Complete the Chapter 5 Study Guide and Review on pages 262–264 of your textbook.

- Complete the Ready to Go On quizzes on pages 242 and 258 of your textbook.

Holt Mathematics

LESSON 6-1 Relating Fractions, Decimals, and Percents

Lesson Objectives

Compare and order fractions, decimals, and percents

Vocabulary

percent (p. 274) _____

_____

Additional Examples

Example 1

Find the missing fraction or percent equivalent for each letter *a–g* on the number line.

$$66\frac{2}{3}\%$$

10% b   40%   d | $87\frac{1}{2}\%$ 125%

a $\frac{1}{4}$ c $\frac{3}{5}$ e   f   g

a: $10\% = \dfrac{\boxed{}}{100} = \boxed{}$

b: $\dfrac{1}{4} = 0.\boxed{} = \boxed{}\%$

c: $40\% = \dfrac{\boxed{}}{100} = \dfrac{\boxed{}}{10} = \boxed{}$

d: $\dfrac{3}{5} = 0.\boxed{} = \boxed{}\%$

e: $66\frac{2}{3}\% = 0.\boxed{} = \boxed{}$

f: $87\frac{1}{2}\% = 0.\boxed{} = \dfrac{\boxed{}}{1000} = \boxed{}$

g: $125\% = \boxed{} = \boxed{} = \boxed{}$

Holt Mathematics

Example 2

Compare. Write <, >, or =.

A. $\frac{1}{4}$ ▮ 40%

$\frac{1}{4} = 0.\boxed{} = \boxed{}$ %   Write as a percent.

$\boxed{}$ % $\boxed{}$ 40%   Compare.

$\frac{1}{4}$ $\boxed{}$ 40%

B. 0.893 ▮ 50%

0.893 = $\boxed{}$ %   Write as a percent.

$\boxed{}$ % $\boxed{}$ 50%   Compare.

0.893 $\boxed{}$ 50%

Example 3

Write 0.075%, $\frac{3}{4}$, 0.41, and 100% in order from least to greatest.

$\frac{3}{4} = \boxed{} = \boxed{}$ %

0.41 = $\boxed{}$ %   Write the numbers in the same form.

$\boxed{}$ % < $\boxed{}$ % < $\boxed{}$ % < $\boxed{}$ %   Compare.

Holt Mathematics

Example 4

Gold that is 24 karat is 100% pure gold. Gold that is 14 karat is 14 parts pure gold and 10 parts another metal, such as copper, zinc, silver, or nickel. What percent of 14 karat gold is pure gold?

$\dfrac{\text{parts pure gold}}{\text{total parts}} \longrightarrow \dfrac{\boxed{}}{\boxed{}} = \dfrac{\boxed{}}{\boxed{}}$ Set up a ratio and simplify.

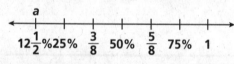

$\dfrac{7}{12} = \boxed{} \div \boxed{} = \boxed{} = \boxed{}\%$ Find the percent.

So 14 karat gold is $\boxed{}$% pure gold.

Check It Out!

1. Find the fraction equivalent for letter *a* on the number line.

a

$12\frac{1}{2}\%\quad 25\%\quad \frac{3}{8}\quad 50\%\quad \frac{5}{8}\quad 75\%\quad 1$

2. Compare. Write <, >, or =.

$\dfrac{3}{4}$ ▇ 65%

3. Write 35%, 0.25, $\frac{1}{2}$, and 200% in order from least to greatest.

4. A baker's dozen is 13. When a shopper purchases a dozen items at the bakery they get 12. It is said that the baker eats 1 item from every batch. What percent of the food does the baker eat?

Holt Mathematics

California Standards NS1.3

LESSON 6-2 Estimating with Percents

Lesson Objectives

Estimate with percents

Vocabulary

estimate (p. 278) _____

_____

compatible numbers (p. 278) _____

_____

Additional Examples

Example 1

Estimate.

21% of 66

21% ≈ 20%   Use a [   ] close to 21%.

≈ [   ]   Write [   ] as a fraction.

66 ≈ 65   Use [   ] numbers,
                   65 and 5.

$\frac{1}{5} \cdot 65 =$ [   ]   Use mental math: 65 ÷ 5.

So 21% of 66 is about [   ].

133

Holt Mathematics

Example 2

PROBLEM SOLVING APPLICATION

Maria took her mother out to lunch for her birthday. The check for lunch
was $20.15. If Maria wants to leave about a 15% tip, about how much
should she pay?

1. **Understand the Problem**

   The answer is the [_____] Maria should pay for their lunch.
   List the important information:

   • The total cost of lunch was $ [_____].

   • Maria wants to leave a [_____] % tip.

2. **Make a Plan**
   Use estimation and mental math to find the tip. Then add the tip to the check
   amount to find the total amount Maria should pay.

3. **Solve**

   First round $20.15 to [_____].   Use compatible numbers.
   $15\% = 10\% + 5\%$ *Think:* 15% is 10% plus 5%.

   10% of $20 = [_____]

   5% of $20 = 10% ÷ 2 = [_____]

   $15\% = 10\% + 5\%$

   = [_____] + [_____] = [_____]

   $20.15 = [_____] = [_____]   Add the tip to the check
                                      amount.

   Maria should pay about [_____].

4. **Look Back**
   Use a calculator to determine whether $3.00 is a reasonable estimate of a
   15% tip.
   $20.15 \cdot 0.15 \approx 3.02$, so $3.00 is a reasonable estimate.

Holt Mathematics

Example 3

A printing company has determined that approximately 6% of the books it prints have errors. Out of a printing run of 2050 books, the production manager estimates that 250 books have errors. Estimate to see if the manager's number is reasonable. Explain.

6% · 2050 ≈ ☐% of ☐ ·   Use ☐.

≈ 0.05 · 2000   Write ☐% as a decimal.

≈ ☐   Multiply.

The manager's estimate is ☐. Only about

100 books have errors.

Check It Out!

Estimate.

29% of 86

2. Fred and Claudia went out to lunch. The total cost of their food was $24.85. If they want to leave a 15% tip, about how much should they pay?

3. A clothing company has determined that approximately 9% of the sheets it makes are irregular. Out of a shipment of 4073, the company manager estimates that 397 sheets are irregular. Estimate to see if the manager's number is reasonable. Explain.

Holt Mathematics

LESSON 6-3

Finding Percents

Lesson Objectives

Find percents

Additional Examples

Example 1

What percent of 92 is 66?

Method 1: Set up a proportion to find the percent.

Think: What number is to 100 as ☐ is to 92?

$\dfrac{\text{number}}{100} = \dfrac{\text{part}}{\text{whole}}$ Set up a ☐.

$\dfrac{n}{100} = \dfrac{\boxed{}}{92}$ Substitute.

$n \cdot 92 = 100 \cdot \boxed{}$ Find the cross ☐.

$92n = \boxed{}$ Simplify.

$n = \dfrac{\boxed{}}{92}$ Divide both sides by 92.

$n \approx \boxed{}$ Simplify.

66 is approximately % of 92.

Method 2: Set up an equation.

percent · whole = part   Set up an equation.

$p \cdot \boxed{} = \boxed{}$ Let p represent the percent.

$\dfrac{92p}{} = \boxed{}$ Divide both sides by ☐.

$p \approx \boxed{}$ Simplify.

66 is about  % of 92.

Holt Mathematics

Example 2

A. Four friends volunteered to cut the grass around their neighbor's house. Jay cut 23% of the grass, Aimee cut $\frac{1}{5}$ of the grass, Ken cut 0.31 of the grass, and Bryn cut the rest. What percent of the grass did Bryn cut?

First, find what percent of the work Jay, Aimee, and Ken did.

$\frac{1}{5}$ = ⬜%, and 0.31 = ⬜%

Next, subtract the percents you know from 100% to find the remaining percent.

100% − ⬜% − ⬜% − ⬜% = ⬜%

Bryn cut ⬜% of the grass.

B. Jeremy organizes his movie collection by genre. $\frac{2}{5}$ of his collection are dramas, 0.325 are action films, 3% are documentaries, 19.5% are comedies, and the rest of his movies are independent films. What percent of his movie collection are independent films?

First, find what percent of his films are dramas and action.

$\frac{2}{5}$ = ⬜% and 0.325 = ⬜%

Next, subtract the percents you know from 100% to find the remaining percent.

100% − ⬜% − ⬜% − ⬜% − ⬜% = ⬜%.

⬜% of Jeremy's movie collection are independent films.

Holt Mathematics

Example 3

A. The city of Dallas, Texas has a population of approximately 1,189,000 people. The population of the city of Austin, Texas is 55% of the population of Dallas. To the nearest thousand, what is the population of Austin?

Choose a method: Set up a proportion.

Think: 55 is to 100 as what population is to 1,189,000?

$$\frac{55}{100} = \frac{p}{\boxed{}}$$ Set up a proportion.

$55 \cdot 1,189,000 = 100 \cdot p$ Find the cross products.

$65,395,000 = 100p$ Simplify.

$\dfrac{65,395,000}{\boxed{}} = \dfrac{100p}{\boxed{}}$ Divide both sides by $\boxed{}$.

$653,950 = p$ Simplify.

$\boxed{} \approx p$ Round to the nearest whole number.

Austin has a population of approximately $\boxed{}$.

B. After a drought, a reservoir had only $66\frac{2}{3}$% of the average amount of water. If the average amount of water is 57,000,000 gallons, how much water was in the reservoir after the drought?

Choose a method: Set up an equation.

Think: What number is $66\frac{2}{3}$% of 57,000,000?

$w = 66\frac{2}{3}\% \cdot \boxed{}$ Set up an equation.

$w = \boxed{} \cdot 57,000,000$ $66\frac{2}{3}$% is equivalent to $\boxed{}$.

$w = \dfrac{114,000,000}{3} = \boxed{}$ Simplify.

The reservoir contained $\boxed{}$ gallons of water after the drought.

Holt Mathematics

Check It Out!

1. What percent of 140 is 21?

2. Four store employees stock the shelves at the Electronics Store. Francisco stocked 14% of the shelves, Lauren stocked $\frac{3}{5}$ of the shelves, Ling stocked 0.19 of the shelves, and Mark stocked the rest. What percent of the shelves did Mark stock?

3. After a drought, a river had only $50\frac{2}{3}\%$ of the average amount of water flow. If the average amount of water flow is 60,000,000 gallons per day, how much water was flowing in the river after the drought?

Holt Mathematics

LESSON 6-4 **Finding a Number When the Percent is Known**

Lesson Objectives

Find a number when the percent is known

Additional Examples

Example 1

60 is 12% of what number?

Choose a method: Set up an equation.

part = percent · whole   Set up an equation.

$60 = 12\% \cdot \boxed{}$ Let n represent the whole.

$60 = 0.12\boxed{}$ $12\% = \boxed{}$

$\boxed{} = \boxed{} n$ Divide both sides by $\boxed{}$.

$\boxed{} = n$ Simplify.

60 is 12% of ▭.

Example 2

Anna earned 85% on a test by answering 17 questions correctly. If each question was worth the same amount, how many questions were on the test?

Choose a method: Set up a proportion.

Think: 85 is to 100 as 17 is to what number?

$\boxed{} = \dfrac{17}{n}$ Set up a $\boxed{}$.

$85 \cdot n = \boxed{} \cdot 17$ Find the cross $\boxed{}$.

$85n = \boxed{}$ Simplify.

$\dfrac{85n}{\boxed{}} = \boxed{}$ Divide both sides by $\boxed{}$.

$n = \boxed{}$ Simplify.

There were ▭ questions on the test.

Holt Mathematics

Example 3

A fisherman caught a lobster that weighed 11.5 lb. This was 70% of the weight of the largest lobster that fisherman had ever caught. What was the weight, to the nearest tenth of a pound, of the largest lobster the fisherman had ever caught?

Choose a method: Set up an equation.

Think: 11.5 is ☐ % of what number?

$11.5 = $ ☐ $\% \cdot n$ Set up an equation.

$11.5 = 0.$☐ $\cdot n$ $70\% = 0.$☐

$\dfrac{☐}{☐} = \dfrac{0.7n}{}$ Divide both sides by ☐.

☐ $\approx n$ Simplify.

The largest lobster the fisherman had ever caught was about ☐ lb.

Check It Out!

1. 75 is 25% of what number?

2. Tom earned 80% on a test by answering 20 questions correctly. If each question was worth the same amount, how many questions were on the test?

3. When Bart was 12, he was approximately 85% of the weight he is now. If Bart was 120 lb, how heavy is he now, to the nearest tenth of a pound?

Holt Mathematics

LESSON
6-5

Applying Percent of Increase and Decrease

Know it!
Note

Lesson Objectives

Find percent of increase and decrease

Vocabulary

percent of change (p. 294) _____

_____

percent of increase (p. 294) _____

_____

percent of decrease (p. 294) _____

_____

discount (p. 295) _____

_____

markup (p. 295) _____

_____

Additional Examples

Example 1

Find the percent increase or decrease from 16 to 12.

This is a percent of decrease.

16 − 12 = ☐   First find the amount of ☐.

$\dfrac{\text{amount of decrease}}{\text{original amount}}$ → $\dfrac{\boxed{}}{16}$ Set up the ratio.

$\dfrac{4}{16}$ = ☐ = ☐ %   Find the decimal form. Write as a percent.

From 16 to 12 is a ☐ % ░░░░░░░░.

Holt Mathematics

Example 2

When Jim was exercising, his heart rate went from 72 beats per minute to 98 beats per minute. What was the percent of increase to the nearest tenth of a percent?

$98 - 72 = \boxed{}$ First find the amount of change.

$\dfrac{\text{amount of increase}}{\text{original amount}} \longrightarrow \dfrac{\boxed{}}{\boxed{}}$ Set up the ratio.

$\dfrac{\boxed{}}{\boxed{}} \approx \boxed{} \approx \boxed{}$%   Find the decimal form. Write as a percent.

From 72 to 98 $\boxed{}$ by about $\boxed{}$%.

Example 3

A. Sarah bought a DVD player originally priced at $450 that was on sale for 20% off. What was the discounted price?

Method 1: Multiply, then subtract.

$(450)(0.\boxed{}) = \boxed{}$ Find $\boxed{}$% of $450.
This is the amount of discount.

$450 - \boxed{} = \boxed{}$ Subtract $\$\boxed{}$ from $450.

Method 2: Subtract, then multiply.

$100\% - 20\% = \boxed{}$%   Find the percent Sarah pays.

$(450)(0.\boxed{}) = \boxed{}$ Find $\boxed{}$% of 450.

The discounted price was $\$\boxed{}$.

Holt Mathematics

B. Mr. Olsen has a computer business in which he sells everything 40% above the wholesale price. If he purchases a printer for $85 wholesale, what will be the retail price?

Method 1: Multiply, then add.

(85)(0.⬚) = ⬚   Find ⬚% of $85.

This is the amount of markup.

85 + ⬚ = ⬚   Add $⬚ to $85.

Method 2: Add, then multiply.

100% + ⬚% = ⬚%   Find the total percent of the selling price.

(85)(⬚) = ⬚   Find ⬚% of 85.

The retail price will be $⬚.

Check It Out!

1. Find the percent of increase or decrease from 50 to 65.

2. In 2005, a certain stock was worth $1.25 a share. In 2006, the same stock was worth $0.85 a share. What was the percent decrease?

3. Lily bought a dog house originally priced at $750 that was on sale for 10% off. What was the sale price?

Holt Mathematics

LESSON
6-6
Commission, Sales Tax, and Profit

Lesson Objectives

Find commission, sales tax, percent of earnings, profit, and total sales

Additional Examples

Example 1

A real-estate agent is paid a monthly salary of $900 plus commission. Last month he sold one condominium for $65,000, earning a 4% commission on the sale. How much was his commission? What was his total pay last month?

First find his commission.

$4\% \cdot \$\boxed{} = c$ commission rate $\cdot$ sales = commission

$0.04 \cdot \boxed{} = c$ Change the percent to a decimal.

$\boxed{} = c$ Solve for c.

He earned a commission of $\$\boxed{}$ on the sale.

Now find his total pay for last month.

$\$\boxed{} + \$\boxed{} = \$\boxed{}$ commission + salary =
total pay

His total pay for last month was $\$\boxed{}$.

Example 2

If the sales tax rate is 6.75%, how much tax would Adrian pay if he bought two CDs at $16.99 each and one DVD for $36.29?

CD: 2 at $16.99 ⟶ $ \boxed{}

DVD: 1 at $36.29 ⟶ $ \boxed{}

$ \boxed{}   Total price

$0.0675 \cdot 70.27 = 4.743225$ Write the tax rate as a decimal and multiply by the total price.

Adrian would pay $\$\boxed{}$ in sales tax.

Holt Mathematics

Example 3

Anna earns $1500 monthly. Of that, $114.75 is withheld for Social Security and Medicare. What percent of Anna's earnings are withheld for Social Security and Medicare?

Think: What percent of $ ☐ is $114.75?

$$\frac{n}{\boxed{}} = \frac{114.75}{\boxed{}}$$ Set up a proportion.

$$n \cdot \boxed{} = \boxed{} \cdot 114.75$$ Find the cross products.

$$\boxed{} = \boxed{}$$ Simplify.

$$\frac{1500}{\boxed{}}\, n = \boxed{}$$ Divide both sides by $\boxed{}$.

$$n = \boxed{}$$ Simplify.

 % of Anna's earnings is withheld for Social Security and Medicare.

Example 4

A furniture store earns 30% profit on all sales. If total sales are $2790, what is the profit?

Think: What is $\boxed{}$ % of 2790?

$$x = \boxed{} \cdot 2790$$ Set up an equation.

$$x = \boxed{}$$ Multiply.

The profit is $ ☐ .

Holt Mathematics

Check It Out!

1. A car sales agent is paid a monthly salary of $700 plus commission. Last month she sold one sports car for $50,000, earning a 5% commission on the sale. How much was her commission? What was her total pay last month?

2. Amy reserves a hotel room for $45 per night. She stays for two nights and pays a sales tax of 13%. How much tax did she pay?

3. BJ earns $2500 monthly. Of that, $500 is withheld for income tax. What percent of BJ's earnings are withheld for income tax?

4. A retail store earns 40% profit on all sales. If total sales are $3320, what is the profit?

Holt Mathematics

LESSON 6-7 Applying Simple and Compound Interest

Lesson Objectives

Compute simple and compound interest

Vocabulary

simple interest (p. 303) _____

_____

principal (p. 303) _____

rate of interest (p. 303) _____

compound interest (p. 304) _____

Additional Examples

Example 1

To buy a car, Jessica borrowed $15,000 for 3 years at an annual simple interest rate of 9%. How much interest will she pay if she pays the entire loan off at the end of the third year? What is the total amount that she will repay?

First, find the interest she will pay.

$I = P \cdot r \cdot t$ Use the formula.

$I = $ [   ] $\cdot$ [   ] $\cdot$ [   ]   Substitute. Use 0.09 for 9%.

$I = $ [   ]   Solve for I.

Jessica will pay $ [   ] in interest.

You can find the total amount A to be repaid on a loan by adding the principal P to the interest I.

$P + I = A$ principal + interest = total amount

[   ] $+$ [   ] $= A$ Substitute.

[   ] $= A$ Solve for A.

Jessica will repay a total of $ [   ] on her loan.

Holt Mathematics

Example 2

Nancy invested $6000 in a bond at a yearly rate of 3%. She earned $450 in interest. How long was the money invested?

$I = P \cdot r \cdot t$ Use the formula.

$\boxed{} = \boxed{} \cdot \boxed{} \cdot t$ Substitute. Use $\boxed{}$ for 3%.

$\boxed{} = \boxed{} \, t$ Simplify.

$\boxed{} = t$ Solve for t.

The money was invested for $\boxed{}$ years, or $\boxed{}$ years $\boxed{}$ months.

Example 3

John's parents deposited $1000 into a savings account as a college fund when he was born. How much will John have in his account after 18 years at a yearly simple interest rate of 3.25%?

$I = P \cdot r \cdot t$ Use the formula.

$I = \boxed{} \cdot \boxed{} \cdot 18$ Substitute. Use $\boxed{}$ for 3.25%

$I = \boxed{}$ Solve for I.

The interest is $\boxed{}$. Now you can find the total.

$P + I = A$ Use the formula.

$\boxed{} + \boxed{} = A$ Substitute.

$\boxed{} = A$ Solve for A.

John will have $\boxed{}$ in the account after 18 years.

Example 4

Mr. Johnson borrowed $8000 for 4 years to make home improvements. If he repaid a total of $10,320, at what interest rate did he borrow the money?

$$P + I = A$$ Use the formula.

$$\boxed{} + I = \boxed{}$$ Substitute.

$$\underline{-\boxed{}} \quad \underline{-\boxed{}}$$ Subtract $\boxed{}$ from both sides.

$$I = \boxed{}$$ Simplify.

He paid $\$\boxed{}$ in interest. Use this amount to find the interest rate.

$$I = P \cdot r \cdot t$$ Use the formula.

$$\boxed{} = \boxed{} \cdot r \cdot \boxed{}$$ Substitute.

$$\boxed{} = \boxed{} r$$ Simplify.

$$\frac{2320}{\boxed{}} = \frac{32{,}000r}{\boxed{}}$$ Divide both sides by $\boxed{}$.

$$\boxed{} = r$$ Simplify.

Mr. Johnson borrowed the money at an annual rate of $\boxed{}$%, or $\boxed{}$%.

Example 5

David invested $1800 in a savings account that pays 4.5% interest compounded semi-annually. Find the value of the investment in 12 years.

$$A = P\left(1 + \frac{r}{n}\right)^{nt}$$ Use the compound interest formula.

$$= \boxed{}\left(1 + \boxed{}\right)^{\boxed{}}$$ Substitute.

$$= \boxed{}\left(1 + \boxed{}\right)^{\boxed{}}$$ Simplify.

$$= \boxed{}\left(\boxed{}\right)^{24}$$ Add inside the parentheses.

Holt Mathematics

= ☐ (☐)   Find $(1.0225)^{24}$ and round.

≈ ☐   Multiply and round to the nearest cent.

After 12 years, the investment will be worth about $ ☐ .

Check It Out!

1. To buy a laptop computer, Elaine borrowed $2,000 for 3 years at an annual simple interest rate of 5%. How much interest will she pay if she pays the entire loan off at the end of the third year? What is the total amount that she will repay?

2. TJ invested $4000 in a bond at a yearly rate of 2%. She earned $200 in interest. How long was the money invested?

3. Bertha deposited $1000 into a retirement account when she was 18. How much will Bertha have in this account after 50 years at a yearly simple interest rate of 7.5%?

4. Mr. Mogi borrowed $9000 for 10 years to make home improvements. If he repaid a total of $20,000 at what interest rate did he borrow the money?

5. Kia invested $3700 in a savings account that pays 2.5% interest compounded quarterly. Find the value of the investment in 10 years.

Holt Mathematics

6-1 Relating Fractions, Decimals, and Percents

Compare. Write <, >, or =.

1. $\frac{1}{5}$ ▇ 25%   2. 0.42 ▇ 41%   3. 0.075 ▇ $7\frac{1}{2}$%

6-2 Estimating with Percents

Estimate.

4. 75% of 195   5. 49% of 19   6. 40% of 219

7. A grade school has 407 students. Approximately 41% of the students walk to school. Estimate how many students walk to school.

6-3 Finding Percents

Find each number to the nearest tenth.

8. What is 35% of 340?   9. What percent of 80 is 18?

10. A son earns 62% of what his father earns. If the son earns $52,000, how much does his father earn to the nearest dollar?

6-4 Finding a Number When the Percent Is Known

Find each number to the nearest whole number.

11. 13 is 52% of what number?   12. 11 is 12.5% of what number?

13. An elephant can run 36% as fast as a cheetah. If a chetah can run 70 mph, how fast can an elephant run to the nearest whole number?

14. A quarterback completed 54% of his passes for the season. If he threw 369 passes in the season, how many passes did he complete to the nearest whole number?

Holt Mathematics

6-5 Applying Percent of Increase and Decrease

Find each percent of increase or decrease to the nearest percent.

15. From 32 to 20

16. From 65 to 130

17. From 142 to 86

18. From 17 to 56

19. A television was marked 30% off. The original price was $1,999. What was the reduced price of the television?

20. Sales at a grocery store increase 22% during the month of December. If the monthly sales are usually $300,000, how much are the sales in December?

6-6 Commission, Sales Tax, and Profit

Find each commission or sales tax to the nearest cent.

21. total sales: $16,000
commission: 3.75%

22. total sales: $21,500
sales tax: 6.75%

23. A realtor earns a 3% commission on each house sold. If a realtor sold two houses for $179,500 and $214,000, what was the total commission?

24. A car salesman earned $918.75 from a commission rate of 3.75% on the sale of a car. What was the price of the car?

6-7 Applying Simple and Compound Interest

Find the interest and total amount to the nearest tenth.

25. $650 at 4.5% per year for 4 years

26. $2,250 at 3% per year for 2 years

27. John borrowed $25,000 to fix his porch. The bank charged him a simple interest rate of 7.75%. How much will John owe if he pays the bank back in 5 years?

Holt Mathematics

Big Ideas

Answer these questions to summarize the important concepts from Chapter 6 in your own words.

1. Explain how to convert $\frac{3}{8}$ to a percent.

2. Explain how to solve "34 is 25% of what number?".

3. Explain how to find the percent of increase or decrease from 200 to 145.

4. Explain how to find the interest and total amount of $400 at 7.5% per year for 8 years.

For more review of Chapter 6:

- Complete the Chapter 6 Study Guide and Review on pages 312–314 of your textbook.

- Complete the Ready to Go On quizzes on pages 292 and 308 of your textbook.

Holt Mathematics

LESSON 7-1
The Coordinate Plane

Lesson Objectives

Plot and identify ordered pairs on a coordinate plane

Vocabulary

coordinate plane (p. 322) _____

_____

x-axis (p. 322) _____

_____

y-axis (p. 322) _____

_____

origin (p. 322) _____

_____

quadrant (p. 322) _____

_____

ordered pair (p. 322) _____

_____

Additional Examples

Example 1

Identify the quadrant that contains each point.

A. *S*

S lies in Quadrant [ ] .

B. *T*

T lies in Quadrant [ ] .

C. *W*

W lies on the [ ] between

Quadrants [ ] and [ ] .

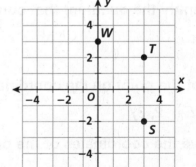

Holt Mathematics

Example 2

Plot each point on a coordinate plane.

A. *D* (3, 3)

Start at the ⬚⬚⬚. Move ⬚ units

right and ⬚ units up.

B. *E* (−2, −3)

Start at the ⬚⬚⬚. Move 2 units

⬚⬚ and 3 units ⬚⬚.

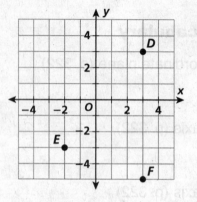

Example 3

Give the coordinates of the point *X*.

Start at the ⬚⬚⬚. Point *X* is ⬚

units left and ⬚ units up.

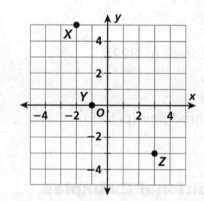

Check It Out!

1. Identify the quadrant that contains the point *X*.

2. Plot the point on the coordinate plane.

E (−2, 3)

3. Give the coordinates of the point *L*.

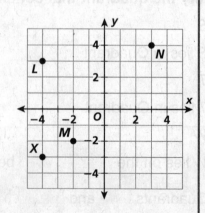

Holt Mathematics

Functions

LESSON 7-2

Lesson Objectives

Represent functions with tables, graphs, or equations

Vocabulary

function (p. 326) _____

_____

input (p. 326) _____

_____

output (p. 326) _____

_____

vertical line test (p. 327) _____

_____

Additional Examples

Example 1

Make a table and a graph of $y = 3 - x^2$.

Make a table of inputs and outputs. Use the table to make a graph.

x	$3 - x^2$	y
−2		
−1		
0		
1		
2		

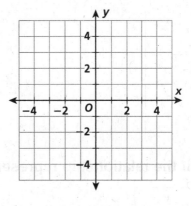

Holt Mathematics

Example 2

Determine if each relationship represents a function.

A.

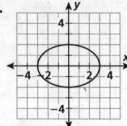

x	2	3	3	2
y	3	4	5	6

The input $x = 2$ has ☐ outputs, $y =$ ☐ and $y =$ ☐.
The input $x = 3$ also has more than one output. The relationship is

☐.

B.

The input $x = 0$ has ☐ outputs,

$y =$ ☐ and $y =$ ☐. Other x-values also

have more than one y-value. The relationship

is ☐.

Check It Out

1. Make a table and a graph of $y = x + 1$.

x	x + 1	y
−1		
0		
1		
2		

2. Determine if the relationship represents a function.

x	y
0	0
1	1
2	2
3	3

Holt Mathematics

LESSON 7-3 **Graphing Linear Functions**

Lesson Objectives

Identify and graph linear equations

Vocabulary

linear equation (p. 330) _____

_____

linear function (p. 330) _____

_____

Additional Examples

Example 1

Graph the linear function $y = 4x - 1$.

Input	Rule	Output	Ordered Pair
x	$4x - 1$	y	(x, y)
0	4(☐) − 1	☐	☐
1	4(☐) − 1	☐	☐
−1	4(☐) − 1	☐	☐

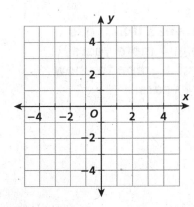

Place each ordered ☐ on the

coordinate grid and then connect the points

with a ☐ .

Holt Mathematics

Example 2

The fastest-moving tectonic plates on Earth move apart at a rate of 15 centimeters per year. Scientists are studying plates that are 30 centimeters apart. Write a linear function that describes the movement of the plates over time. Then make a graph to show the movement over 4 years.

The function is [   ], where x is the number of years and y is the spread in centimeters.

Input	Rule	Output
x	$15x + 30$	y
0	15( ) + 30	
2	15( ) + 30	
4	15( ) + 30	

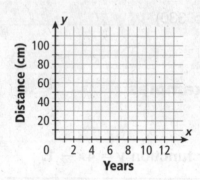

Check It Out!

1. Graph the linear function $y = 3x + 1$.

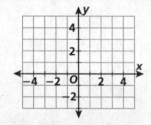

2. Dogs are considered to age 7 years for each human year. If a dog is 3 years old today, how old in human years will it be in 4 more years? Write a linear equation to show this relationship, and a graph to show how the dog will age in human years over the next 4 years.

Holt Mathematics

LESSON 7-4

Graphing Quadratic Functions

Lesson Objectives

Identify and graph quadratic functions

Vocabulary

quadratic function (p. 334) _____

_____

parabola (p. 334) _____

_____

Additional Examples

Example 1

Create a table for the quadratic function, and use it to graph the function.

$y = x^2 + 1$

x	$x^2 + 1$	y
-2		
-1		
0		
1		
2		

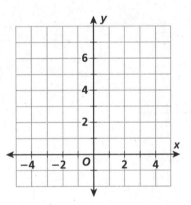

Plot the points and connect them with a smooth curve.

Holt Mathematics

Example 2

A reflecting surface of a television antenna was formed by rotating the parabola $f(x) = 0.1x^2$ about its axis of symmetry. If the antenna has a diameter of 4 feet, about how much higher are the sides than the center?

First create a table of values. Then graph the reflecting surface.

x	$f(x)$
-2	$0.1\ (\boxed{})^2 = \boxed{}$
-1	$0.1\ (\boxed{})^2 = \boxed{}$
0	$0.1\ (\boxed{})^2 = \boxed{}$
1	$0.1\ (\boxed{})^2 = \boxed{}$
2	$0.1\ (\boxed{})^2 = \boxed{}$

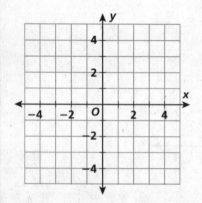

The center of the antenna is at $x = \boxed{}$, and the height is $\boxed{}$ ft. If the diameter of the antenna is 4 ft, the highest point on the side is at $x = \boxed{}$.

The height is $f(\boxed{}) = 0.1(\boxed{})^2 = \boxed{}$ ft. The sides are about $\boxed{}$ ft higher than the center.

Holt Mathematics

Check It Out!

1. Create a table for each quadratic function, and use it to make a graph.

$y = x^2 - 1$

2. A reflecting surface of a radio antenna was formed by rotating the parabola $y = x^2 - x + 2$ about its axis of symmetry. If the antenna has a diameter of 3 feet, about how much higher are the sides than the center?

Holt Mathematics

**LESSON
7-5**

Cubic Functions

Lesson Objectives

Identify and graph cubic functions

Vocabulary

cubic function (p. 338) _____

_____

Additional Examples

Example 1

Create a table for each quadratic function, and use it to graph the function.

$y = x^3 - 2$

x	$x^3 - 2$	y
−2		
−1		
0		
1		
2		

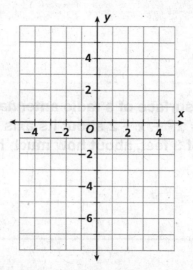

Example 2

Tell whether the function is linear, quadratic, or cubic.

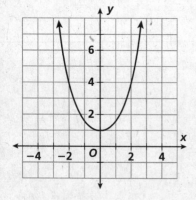

The graph is a [   ],

so it is a [   ] function.

Holt Mathematics

Check It Out!

1. Create a table for each cubic function, and use it to graph the function.

$y = -x^3 - 1$

2. Tell whether the function is linear, quadratic, or cubic.

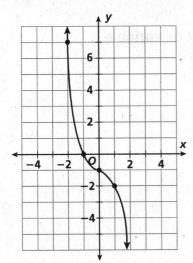

Rate of Change and Slope

LESSON 7-6

Lesson Objectives

Find rates of change and slopes

Vocabulary

rate of change (p. 344) _____

_____

rise (p. 344) _____

_____

run (p. 344) _____

_____

slope (p. 345) _____

_____

Additional Examples

Example 1

Determine whether the rates of change are constant or variable.

Find the differences between consecutive data points.

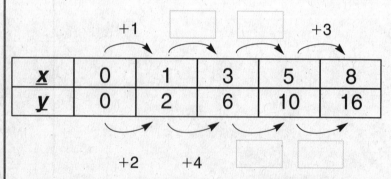

Find each ratio of change in y to change in x.

$$\frac{\square}{\square} = 2 \qquad \frac{4}{\square} = \square \qquad \frac{\square}{2} = 2 \qquad \frac{\square}{3} = \square$$

The rates of change are _____ .

Holt Mathematics

Example 2

Find the slope of the line.

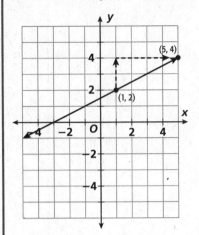

Begin at one point and count vertically to find the rise.

Then count horizontally to the second point to find the run.

slope $= \dfrac{\boxed{}}{\boxed{}} = \dfrac{\boxed{}}{\boxed{}}$

The slope of the line is $\boxed{}$.

Example 3

Find the value of *a*.

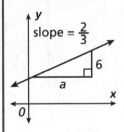

slope $= \dfrac{\boxed{}}{\boxed{}}$

$\dfrac{\boxed{}}{3} = \dfrac{6}{\boxed{}}$ Cross multiply.

$2a = \boxed{} \cdot 6$ Multiply.

$2a = \boxed{}$ Divide both sides by 2.

$a = \boxed{}$

Holt Mathematics

Check It Out!

1. Determine whether the rates of change are constant or variable.

x	0	1	4	6	9
y	0	2	8	12	18

2. Find the slope of the line.

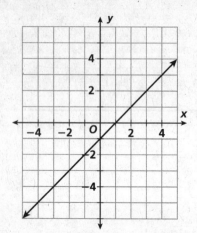

3. Find the value of *a*.

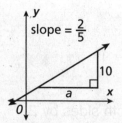

Holt Mathematics

LESSON 7-7

Finding Slope of a Line

Lesson Objectives

Find the slope of a line and use slope to understand graphs

Additional Examples

Example 1

Find the slope of the line that passes through $(-2, -3)$ and $(4, 6)$.

Let (x_1, y_1) be $(-2, -3)$ and (x_2, y_2) be $(4, 6)$.

$$\frac{y_2 - y_1}{x_2 - x_1} = \frac{\boxed{} - (\boxed{})}{\boxed{} - \boxed{}} = \boxed{} = \boxed{}$$

The slope of the line is $\boxed{}$.

Example 2

The table shows the total cost of fruit per pound purchased at the grocery store. Use the data to make a graph. Find the slope of the line and explain what it shows.

Cost of Fruit	
Pounds	**Cost**
0	0
5	15
10	30
15	45

Plot the data points and connect them.

Put $\boxed{}$ on the x-axis

and $\boxed{}$ on the y-axis.

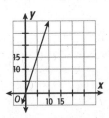

Find the slope of the line.

$$m = \frac{y_2 - y_1}{x_2 - x_1} = \frac{15 - 0}{5 - 0} = \frac{15}{5} = \boxed{}$$

Substitute 15 for y_2, 0 for y_1, 5 for x_2, and 0 for x_1.

The slope of the line is $\boxed{}$. This means for every pound of fruit, you will

pay another $\$\boxed{}$.

Holt Mathematics

Check It Out!

1. Find the slope of the line that passes through (−4, −6) and (2, 3).

2. The table shows the total cost of gas per gallon. Use the data to make a graph. Find the slope of the line and explain what it shows.

Cost of Gas	
Gallons	Cost
0	0
3	6
6	12

Holt Mathematics

LESSON 7-8

Interpreting Graphs

Lesson Objectives

Relate graphs to situations

Additional Examples

Example 1

The height of a tree increases over time, but not at a constant rate. Which graph bests shows this?

a.

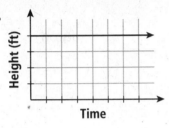

b.

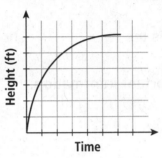

As the tree grows, its height [_____] and then reaches its

[_____] height. Graph [___] shows the height of a tree not increasing

but remaining constant. Graph [___] shows the height of a tree increasing but

not at a constant rate. The answer is graph [___].

Holt Mathematics

Example 2

Jarod parked his car in the supermarket parking lot and walked 40 ft into the store to the customer service counter, where he waited in line to pay his electric bill. Jarod then walked 60 ft to the back of the store to get 2 gallons of milk and walked 50 ft to the checkout near the front of the store to pay for them. After waiting his turn and paying for the milk, he walked 50 ft back to his car. Sketch a graph to show Jarod's distance from his car over time.

1. Understand the Problem

The answer is the [_____] showing [_____] Jarod traveled.

List the **important information**:

• Jarod walked to the [_____].

• Jarod [_____] in line.

• Jarod walked to the [_____] of the store.

• Jarod walked to the [_____].

• Jarod [_____] in line.

• Jarod went back to his [_____].

2. Make a Plan

The distance [_____] as Jarod walks to the customer service counter. The distance [_____] when Jarod waits in line. The distance [_____] as Jarod walks to the back of the store. The distance [_____] as Jarod walks to the checkout. The distance [_____] when Jarod waits in line. The distance [_____] as Jarod walks back to his car.

Holt Mathematics

3. Solve

Sketch a graph of the situation.

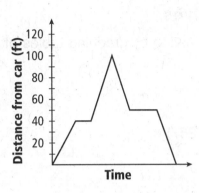

4. Look Back

The graph is reasonable because it pictures someone walking away, standing still, walking away, walking back, standing in line, and walking back.

Check It Out!

1. The dimensions of the basketball court have changed over the years. However, the height of the basket has not changed. Which graph bests shows this?

a.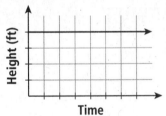

b.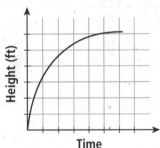

2. Darcy traveled 22 miles from her house to the Peterman's house where she babysat for 1 hour. After babysitting she traveled 8 miles further to the deli to buy a sandwich. After eating her sandwich she returned home. Sketch a graph to show Darcy's distance from her house over time.

Holt Mathematics

LESSON 7-9 **Direct Variation**

Lesson Objectives

Recognize direct variation by graphing tables of data and checking for constant ratios

Vocabulary

direct variation (p. 357) _____

_____

constant of variation (p. 357) _____

_____

Additional Examples

Example 1

Determine whether the data set shows direct variation.

A.

Adam's Growth Chart				
Age (mo)	3	6	9	12
Length (in.)	22	24	25	27

Make a graph that shows the relationship between Adam's age and his length.

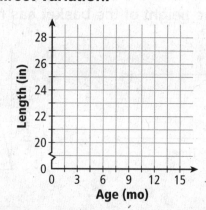

You can also compare ratios to see if a direct [_____] occurs.

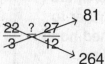

81   [____] ≠ [____]

264   The ratios are [_____].

The relationship of the data is [_____].

Holt Mathematics

Example 2

Rachel rents space in a salon to cut and style hair. She paid the owner $24 for 3 cut and styles. Write a direct variation function for this situation. If Rachel does 7 cut and styles, how much will she pay the owner?

$y = kx$ — Write the direct variation function. y is the amount owed, and x is the number of cuts given.

$\boxed{} = k \cdot 3$ — Substitute $\boxed{}$ for y and 3 for $\boxed{}$.

$\boxed{} = k$ — Solve for k.

$y = \boxed{}\, x$ — Substitute $\boxed{}$ for k in the original equation.

$y = 8(\boxed{})$ — Substitute $\boxed{}$ for x in the direct variation function.

$y = \boxed{}$ — Multiply.

Rachel will pay the salon owner $\boxed{}$ for 7 cut and styles.

Example 3

Mrs. Perez has $4000 in a CD. The amount of interest she has earned since the beginning of the year is organized in the following table. Determine whether there is a direct variation between the data set and time. If so, find the equation of direct variation.

Time (mo)	Interest from CD ($)
0	0
1	17
2	34
3	51
4	68

$$\frac{\text{interest from CD}}{\text{time}} = \frac{\boxed{}}{1} = \frac{34}{\boxed{}} = \frac{51}{\boxed{}} = \frac{\boxed{}}{4} = \boxed{}$$

The variables are related by a constant ratio of $\boxed{}$ to $\boxed{}$.

Holt Mathematics

Check It Out!

1. Determine whether the data set shows direct variation.

Kyle's Basketball Shots			
Distance (ft)	20	30	40
Number of Baskets	5	3	0

2. Rinny cuts and styles hair in a salon. She earns $120 for 4 cut and styles. Write a direct variation function for this situation. If Rinny does 9 cut and styles, how much will she earn?

3. Mr. Ortega has $2000 in a CD and $2000 in a money market account. The amount of interest he has earned since the beginning of the year is organized in the following table. Determine whether there is a direct variation between either of the data sets and time. If so, find the equation of direct variation.

Time (mo)	Interest from CD ($)	Interest from Money Market ($)
0	0	0
1	12	15
2	30	40
3	40	45
4	50	50

Holt Mathematics

Know it!
.Note

7-1 The Coordinate Plane

Identify the quadrant that contains each point.

1. (7, 3)

2. (−5, −1)

3. (−3, 0)

4. (2, −2)

Plot each ordered pair on a coordinate plane.

5. (3, −5)

6. (0, 4)

7. (−1, 6)

8. (4, 2)

7-2 Functions

9. Make a table and a graph of $y = x^2 - 2$.

Determine if each relationship is a function.

10.

x	y
1	11
1	27
9	43
16	71

11.

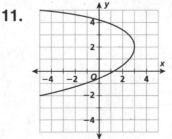

12. $y = -5x^2 + 7$

Holt Mathematics

7-3 Graphing Linear Functions

Graph each linear function.

13. $y = 3x - 2$

14. $y = -2x + 4$

7-4 Graphing Quadratic Functions

Create a table for each quadratic function, and use it to graph the function.

15. $y = 3x^2$

16. $y = x^2 + x + 1$

Holt Mathematics

7-5 Cubic Functions

Create a table for the cubic function, and use it to graph the function.

17. $x^3 - 3$

18. Tell whether the function in linear, quadratic, or cubic.

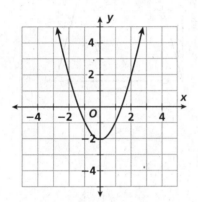

7-6 Rate of Change and Slope

Determine whether the rates of change are constant or variable.

19.

x	0	3	9	12	15
y	4	6	10	12	14

20.

x	1	5	7	10	12
y	4	10	13	15	18

21. Find the slope of the line.

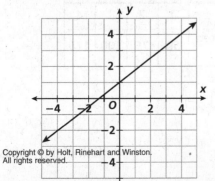

Holt Mathematics

7-7 Slope of a Line

Find the slope of the line that passes through each pair of points.

22. $(-4, -5)$ and $(2, 4)$ **23.** $(-4, 4)$ and $(1, 3)$ **24.** $(3, 2)$ and $(4, 6)$

7-8 Interpreting Graphs

25. An airplane increases in altitude from take-off until it reaches its cruising altitude. It flies at the cruising altitude until it begins to descend for landing. Which graph best shows the story?

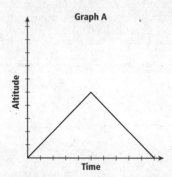

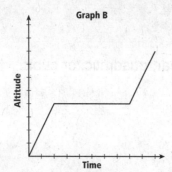

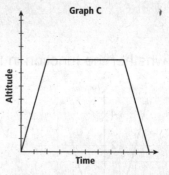

26. Nolan rode his bike to school. After school he rode his bike to a friend's house. Then he rode his bike home. Sketch a graph to show the distance Nolan traveled.

7-9 Direct Variation

Determine whether the data set shows direct variation.

27.

Plant Growth Chart				
Age (weeks)	2	4	6	8
Height (cm)	3	6	9	12

28.

Tino's Charity Collections Chart				
Time (hours)	1	2	3	4
Money collected (dollars)	50	75	100	125

Holt Mathematics

Answer these questions to summarize the important concepts from Chapter 7 in your own words.

1. How can you tell if a relationship is a function?

2. Describe the ways in which a linear function looks different from a quadratic function and a cubic function.

3. What is the rate of change, and how is it like the slope of a line?

4. If the points (1, 7) and (9, 8) are on a line, how do you find the slope?

5. What are two ways that you can see if a set has direct variation?

For more review of Chapter 7:

• Complete the Chapter 7 Study Guide and Review on pages 366–368 of your textbook.

• Complete the Ready to Go On quizzes on pages 342 and 362 of your textbook.

Holt Mathematics

Points, Lines, Planes, and Angles

Lesson Objectives

Classify and name figures

Vocabulary

point (p. 378) _____

line (p. 378) _____

_____

plane (p. 378) _____

segment (p. 378) _____

ray (p. 378) _____

_____

angle (p. 379) _____

_____

acute angle (p. 379) _____

_____

right angle (p. 379) _____

obtuse angle (p. 379) _____

_____

straight angle (p. 379) _____

complementary angles (p. 379) _____

_____

supplementary angles (p. 379) _____

_____

Holt Mathematics

Additional Examples

Example 1

Use the diagram to name each figure.

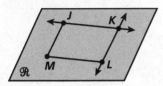

A. a line

Any ☐ points on a line can be used.

B. a plane

Any ☐ points in the plane that form a triangle can be used.

C. four segments

Write the 2 points in any order, for example ☐ or ☐.

D. four rays

Write the ☐ first.

Holt Mathematics

Example 2

Use the diagram to name each figure.

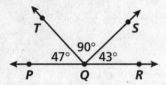

A. a right angle

B. two acute angles

C. two obtuse angles

m∠SQP = [ ]°, m∠RQT = [ ]°

D. a pair of complementary angles

m∠TQP + m∠RQS = [ ]° + [ ]° = 90°

E. two pairs of supplementary angles

m∠TQP + m∠TQR = [ ]° + [ ]° = 180°

m∠SQP + m∠SQR = [ ]° + [ ]° = 180°

Check It Out!

1. Use the diagram to name four segments.

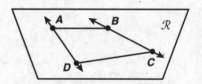

2. Use the diagram to name two acute angles.

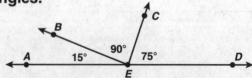

Holt Mathematics

LESSON 8-2 **Geometric Relationships**

Lesson Objectives

Describe how lines and planes are related in space

Vocabulary

parallel lines (p. 384) _____

perpendicular lines (p. 384) _____

skew lines (p. 384) _____

parallel planes (p. 385) _____

perpendicular planes (p. 385) _____

Additional Examples

Example 1

Identify two lines that have the given relationship.

A. parallel lines   The lines are in the same [_____] and do not

[_____] [_____].

B. perpendicular lines   The lines intersect to form [____]° angles.

[_____]

C. skew lines   The lines lie in different [_____].

[_____]

Holt Mathematics

Example 2

Identify two planes that appear to have the given relationship.

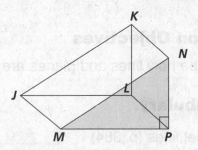

A. perpendicular planes

The planes intersect to form [____] angles.

B. parallel planes

The planes do not [____].

C. neither perpendicular nor parallel planes

The planes [____], but do not form [____] angles.

Check It Out!

1. Identify two lines that have the given relationship.

skew lines

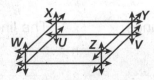

2. Identify two planes that appear to have the given relationship.

parallel planes

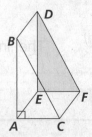

Holt Mathematics

Angle Relationships

Lesson Objectives

Identify parallel and perpendicular lines and the angles formed by a transversal

Additional Examples

Example 1

Use the diagram to find each angle measure.

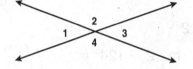

A. If m∠1 = 37°, find m∠3.

m∠2 = 180° − ☐ = 143°   ∠1 and ∠2 are

☐.

m∠3 = 180° − ☐ = 37°   The measures of ∠2 and ∠3 are

☐.

So m∠1 = m∠3.

B. If m∠4 = $y°$, find m∠2.

m∠3 = 180° − $y°$ ∠3 and ∠4 are

☐.

m∠2 = 180° − m∠3   ∠2 and ∠3 are

☐.

= 180° − (☐)   Substitute 180° − $y°$ for ☐.

= 180° − 180° + $y°$ Distributive Property

= ☐   Simplify.

So m∠4 = m∠2.

Holt Mathematics

Example 2

In the figure, line *l* ∥ line *m*.
Find the measure of each angle.

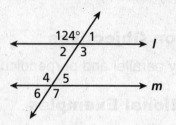

A. ∠4

m∠4 = [____]°

All obtuse angles in

the figure are [_____].

B. ∠2

m∠2 + 124° = [_____]°   ∠2 is [_____] to

the angle 124°.

[_____]° [_____]°

m∠2 = [_____]°

C. ∠6

m∠6 = [_____]   ∠2 and ∠6 are [_____]

angles.

Check It Out!

1. Use the diagram to find the angle measure.

If m∠1 = 42°, find m∠3.

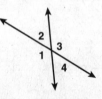

2. In the figure, line *n* ∥ line *m*. Find the measure of the angle.

∠1

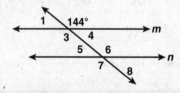

Holt Mathematics

California Standards ← MG3.3, Rev. of ← 6MG2.2

LESSON 8-4

Triangles

Lesson Objectives

Find unknown angles in triangles

Vocabulary

Triangle Sum Theorem (p. 392) _____

_____

acute triangle (p. 392) _____

_____

right triangle (p. 392) _____

_____

obtuse triangle (p. 392) _____

_____

equilateral triangle (p. 393) _____

_____

isosceles triangle (p. 393) _____

_____

scalene triangle (p. 393) _____

_____

midpoint (p. 393) _____

_____

altitude (p. 393) _____

_____

Additional Examples

Example 1

A. Find *p* in the acute triangle.

$$\boxed{}^{\circ} + \boxed{}^{\circ} + p = \boxed{}^{\circ} \qquad \text{Sum Theorem}$$

$$\boxed{}^{\circ} + p = \boxed{}$$

$$\underline{\quad -117 \qquad\qquad -117\quad} \qquad \text{Subtract } \boxed{} \text{ from both sides.}$$

$$p = \boxed{}$$

B. Find *m* in the obtuse triangle.

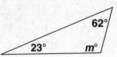

$$\boxed{}^{\circ} + \boxed{}^{\circ} + m^{\circ} = \boxed{}^{\circ} \qquad \text{Triangle Sum Theorem}$$

$$\boxed{}^{\circ} + m = \boxed{}$$

$$\underline{\quad -85 \qquad\qquad -85\quad} \qquad \text{Subtract } \boxed{} \text{ from each side.}$$

$$m = \boxed{}$$

Example 2

Find the angle measures in the isosceles triangle.

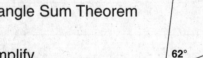
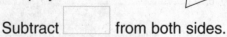

$$62^{\circ} + t^{\circ} + t^{\circ} = \boxed{}^{\circ} \qquad \text{Triangle Sum Theorem}$$

$$62 + \boxed{} = \boxed{} \qquad \text{Simplify.}$$

$$\underline{\quad -62 \qquad\qquad -62\quad} \qquad \text{Subtract } \boxed{} \text{ from both sides.}$$

$$2t = \boxed{}$$

$$\frac{2t}{\boxed{}} = \frac{118}{\boxed{}} \qquad \boxed{} \text{ both sides by } \boxed{}.$$

$$t = \boxed{}$$

The angles labeled t° measure $\boxed{}^{\circ}$.

Holt Mathematics

Example 3

The second angle in a triangle is six times as large as the first. The third angle is half as large as the second. Find the angle measures and draw a possible picture.

Let $x° =$ the first angle measure. Then $6x° =$ second angle measure, and $\frac{1}{2}(6x°) = 3x° =$ third angle measure.

$x° + 6x° + 3x° = \boxed{}°$ Triangle $\boxed{}$ Theorem

$\dfrac{10x°}{\boxed{}} = \dfrac{180°}{\boxed{}}$ Simplify. Divide both sides by $\boxed{}$.

$x° = \boxed{}°$

The angles measure $\boxed{}°$, $\boxed{}°$, and $\boxed{}°$.

The triangle is an obtuse $\boxed{}$ triangle.

Check It Out!

1. Find *a* in the acute triangle.

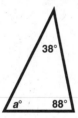

2. Find the angle measures in the scalene triangle.

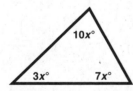

3. The second angle in a triangle is three times larger than the first. The third angle is one third as large as the second. Find the angle measures and draw a possible picture.

Holt Mathematics

LESSON 8-5

Coordinate Geometry

Lesson Objectives

Identify polygons in the coordinate plane

Vocabulary

polygon (p. 399) _____

_____

quadrilateral (p. 399) _____

trapezoid (p. 399) _____

_____

parallelogram (p. 399) _____

_____

rectangle (p. 399) _____

rhombus (p. 399) _____

square (p. 399) _____

_____

Additional Examples

Example 1

Which lines are parallel?
Which lines are perpendicular?

slope of $\overleftrightarrow{EF}$ = $\dfrac{3}{\boxed{}}$

slope of $\overleftrightarrow{GH}$ = $\dfrac{3}{\boxed{}}$

slope of $\overleftrightarrow{PQ}$ = $\dfrac{3}{\boxed{}}$

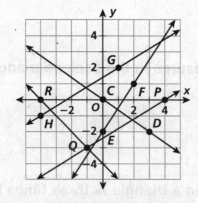

Holt Mathematics

slope of $\overleftrightarrow{CD}$ = $\dfrac{\boxed{}}{\boxed{}}$ or $\boxed{}$

slope of $\overleftrightarrow{QR}$ = $\dfrac{\boxed{}}{\boxed{}}$ or -1

$\boxed{}$ ‖ $\boxed{}$ The slopes are $\boxed{}$. $\dfrac{3}{5} = \dfrac{3}{5}$

$\boxed{}$ ⊥ $\boxed{}$ The slopes have a $\boxed{}$ of -1: $\dfrac{3}{2} \cdot -\dfrac{2}{3} = -1$

Example 2

Graph the quadrilateral with the given vertices. Give all of the names that apply to the quadrilateral.

$A(3, -2)$, $B(2, -1)$, $C(4, 3)$, $D(5, 2)$

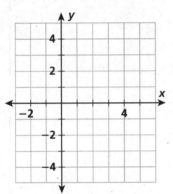

$\overline{BC} \parallel \overline{AD}$ and $\overline{BA} \parallel \overline{CD}$

Example 3

Find the coordinates of the missing vertex.

Rectangle $WXYZ$ with $W(-2, 2)$, $X(3, 2)$, and $Y(3, -4)$

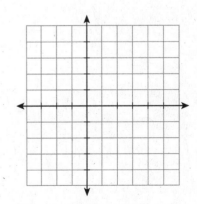

Step 1: Graph and connect the given points.

Step 2: Complete the figure to find the missing vertex.

The coordinates of **Z** are $\boxed{}$.

Holt Mathematics

LESSON 8-5 *CONTINUED*

Check It Out!

1. **Which lines are parallel? Which lines are perpendicular?**

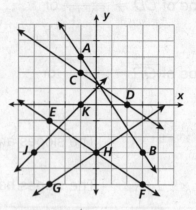

2. **Graph the quadrilateral with the given vertices. Give all the names that apply to the quadrilateral.**

   $R(-3, 1)$, $S(-4, 2)$, $T(-3, 3)$, $U(-2, 2)$

3. **Find the coordinates of the missing vertex.**

   Rectangle *JKLM* with $J(-1, 2)$, $K(4, 2)$, and $L(4, -1)$

Holt Mathematics

LESSON 8-6 **Congruent Polygons**

Lesson Objectives

Use properties of congruent figures to solve problems

Vocabulary

correspondence (p. 406) _____

_____

congruent (p. 406) _____

_____

Additional Examples

Example 1

Write a congruence statement for the pair of polygons.

A.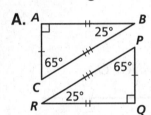

The first triangle can be named triangle *ABC*. To complete the congruence statement, the vertices in the second triangle have to be written in

[_____] of the [_____].

∠*A* ≅ ∠[___], so ∠*A* corresponds to ∠[___].

∠*B* ≅ ∠[___], so ∠*B* corresponds to ∠[___].

∠*C* ≅ ∠[___], so ∠*C* corresponds to ∠[___].

The congruence statement is triangle [_____] ≅ triangle [_____].

Holt Mathematics

B.

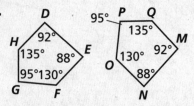

The vertices in the first pentagon are written in order around the pentagon starting at any vertex.

$\angle D$ corresponds to ☐. $\angle D \cong \angle M$

$\angle E$ corresponds to ☐. $\angle E \cong \angle N$

$\angle F$ corresponds to ☐. $\angle F \cong \angle O$

$\angle G$ corresponds to ☐. $\angle G \cong \angle P$

$\angle H$ corresponds to ☐. $\angle H \cong \angle Q$

The congruence statement is pentagon *DEFGH* $\cong$ pentagon *MNOPQ*.

Example 2

In the figure, quadrilateral *VWXY* $\cong$ quadrilateral *JKLM*.

A. Find *a*.

$a + 8 = 24$
$\underline{-8 \quad -8}$ $\overline{WX} \cong$ ☐   Subtract 8 from both sides.

$a \quad =$ ☐

B. Find *b*.

$6b = 30$ $\overline{ML} \cong$ ☐

   Divide both sides by 6.

$b =$ ☐

Holt Mathematics

C. Find c.

$5c = 85$ $\angle\boxed{} \approx \angle\boxed{}$

$\dfrac{5c}{5} = \dfrac{85}{5}$ Divide both sides by 5.

$c = \boxed{}$

Check It Out!

1. Write a congruence statement for the pair of polygons.

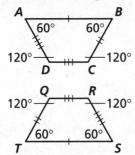

2. In the figure, quadrilateral $JIHK \cong$ quadrilateral $QRST$. Find c.

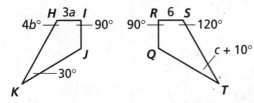

Holt Mathematics

Transformations

Lesson Objectives

Recognize, describe, and show transformations

Vocabulary

transformation (p. 410) _____

_____

image (p. 410) _____

_____

translation (p. 410) _____

_____

reflection (p. 410) _____

_____

rotation (p. 410) _____

Additional Examples

Example 1

Identify each type of transformation.

A.

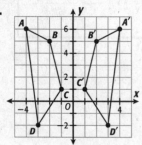

B.

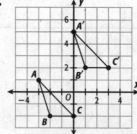

Holt Mathematics

Example 2

Graph the translation of quadrilateral *ABCD* 4 units left and 2 down.

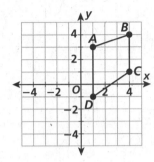

Each vertex is moved 4 units

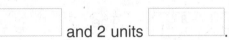 and 2 units _____.

Example 3

Graph the reflection of the figure across the indicated axis. Write the coordinates of the vertices of the image.

A. *x*-axis

The *x*-coordinates of the corresponding

vertices are _____, and the

y-coordinates of the corresponding vertices

are _____.

The coordinates of the vertices of triangle *A′D′C′* are

_____

B. *y*-axis

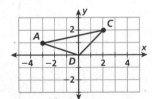

The *y*-coordinates of the corresponding

vertices are _____, and the

x-coordinates of the corresponding vertices

are _____.

The coordinates of the vertices of triangle *A′D′C′* are

_____

Holt Mathematics

Example 4

Triangle *ABC* has vertices *A*(1, 0), *B*(3, 3), *C*(5, 0). Rotate △*ABC* 180° about the vertex *A*.

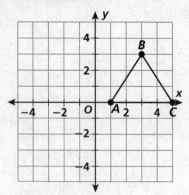

The ⬚⬚⬚⬚⬚⬚⬚⬚⬚⬚⬚⬚

sides, $\overline{AC}$ and $\overline{A'C'}$, make a

180° angle.

Notice that the vertex *C* is ⬚ units to the ⬚⬚⬚⬚⬚ of vertex *A*, and

vertex *C'* is ⬚ units to the ⬚⬚⬚⬚⬚ of vertex *A*.

Check It Out!

1. Identify the type of transformation.

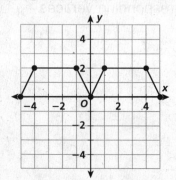

2. Graph the translation of quadrilateral *ABCD* 5 units left and 3 units down.

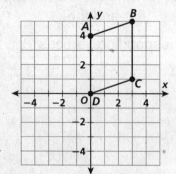

Holt Mathematics

3. Graph the reflection of the figure across the *y*-axis. Write the coordinates of the vertices of the image.

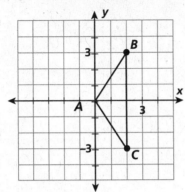

4. Triangle *ABC* has vertices *A*(−2, 0), *B*(0, 3), *C*(0, −3). Rotate △*ABC* 180° about the vertex *A*.

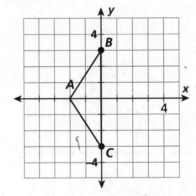

Holt Mathematics

Tessellations

LESSON
8-8

Lesson Objectives

Create tessellations.

Vocabulary

tessellation (p. 416) _____

_____

regular tessellation (p. 416) _____

_____

Additional Examples

Example 1

Create a tessellation with quadrilateral *EFGH*.

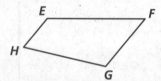

There must be a copy of each angle of
quadrilateral *EFGH* at every vertex.

Example 2

Use rotations to create a variation of the tessellation in Additional Example 1.

Step 1: Find the midpoint of a side.

Step 2: Make a new edge for half of the side.

Step 3: Rotate the new edge around the midpoint to form the edge of the
other half of the side.

Step 4: Repeat with the other sides.

Step 5: Use the figure to make a tessellation.

Holt Mathematics

Check It Out!

1. Create a tessellation with quadrilateral *IJKL*.

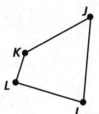

2. Use rotations to create a tessellation with the quadrilateral given below.

Holt Mathematics

8-1 Points, Lines, Planes, and Angles

Use the diagram to name each geometric figure.

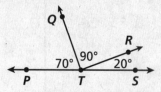

1. two obtuse angles

2. two segments

8-2 Geometric Relationships

Use the figure to identify the following.

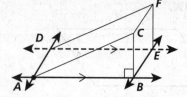

3. two parallel lines

4. two perpendicular lines

5. two perpendicular planes

8-3 Angle Relationships

In the figure, line *a* ∥ line *b*.

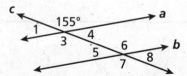

6. Find the measure of ∠6.

7. Find the measure of ∠8.

8. Which line is the transversal?

9. Name three pairs of supplementary angles.

Holt Mathematics

8-4 Triangles

Find the value of each variable.

10.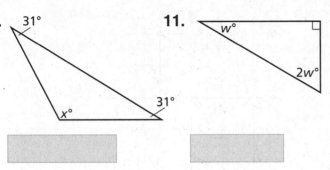

11.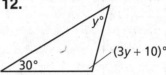

12.

8-5 Coordinate Geometry

13. Which lines are parallel?

14. Which lines are perpendicular?

15. Find the coordinates of the missing vertex of rectangle *ABCD* with *A*(5, 4), *B*(9, 4), and *C*(9, 2).

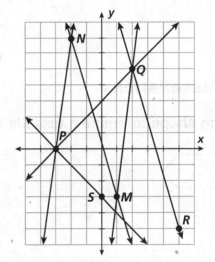

8-6 Congruent Polygons

Write a congruence statement for each pair of polygons.

16.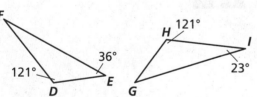

17.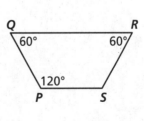

Holt Mathematics

8-7 Transformations

Identify each type of transformation.

18.
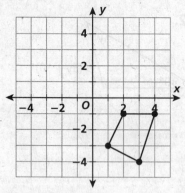

19.
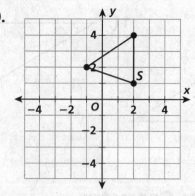

8-8 Tessellations

Use the shape to create a tessellation.

20.

21. A piece is removed from one side of a square and translated to the opposite side. Will this shape tessellate?

Holt Mathematics

Answer these questions to summarize the important concepts from Chapter 8 in your own words.

1. Explain the difference between complementary angles and supplementary angles.

2. If ∠1 is 50°, explain how to find m∠5.

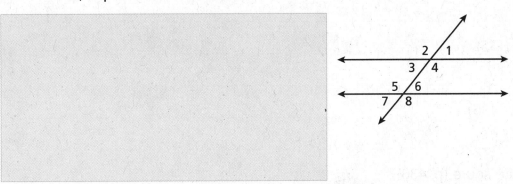

3. If the measures of two angles in a triangle are 43° and 74°, explain how to find the measure of the third angle.

4. Explain how to use rotations to create a variation of a tessellation.

For more review of Chapter 8:

• Complete the Chapter 8 Study Guide: Review on pages 424–426 of your textbook.

• Complete the Ready to Go On quizzes on pages 404 and 420 of your textbook.

Holt Mathematics

LESSON 9-1 **Perimeter & Area of Parallelograms**

Lesson Objectives

Find the perimeter and area of parallelograms

Vocabulary

perimeter (p. 434) _____

_____

area (p. 435) _____

_____

base (p. 435) _____

_____

height (p. 435) _____

_____

composite figure (p. 436) _____

_____

Additional Examples

Example 1

Find the perimeter of the parallelogram.

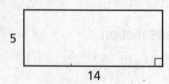

$P = \boxed{} + \boxed{} + \boxed{} + \boxed{}$ Add all side lengths.

$= \boxed{}$ units

or $P = 2b + 2h$ Perimeter of rectangle

$= 2(\boxed{}) + 2(\boxed{})$ Substitute $\boxed{}$ for b and $\boxed{}$ for h.

$= 28 + 10 = \boxed{}$ units

Holt Mathematics

Example 2

Graph and find the area of the figure with the given vertices.

$(-1, -2)$, $(2, -2)$, $(2, 3)$, $(-1, 3)$

$A = bh$ Area of a rectangle

$= \boxed{} \cdot \boxed{}$ Substitute $\boxed{}$ for b and $\boxed{}$ for h.

$= \boxed{}$ units²

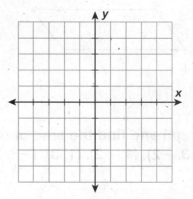

Example 3

Find the perimeter and area of the figure.

```
     6        6
  ┌──────┐ 3 ┌──────┐
5 │   3 └─6─┘ 3   │ 5
  └──────────────┘
```

The length of the side that is not labeled is the same as the total length of

the opposite side, or $\boxed{} + \boxed{} + \boxed{}$, which equals $\boxed{}$.

$P = \boxed{} + \boxed{} + \boxed{} + \boxed{} + \boxed{} + \boxed{} + \boxed{} + \boxed{}$

$= \boxed{}$ units

```
       6                        6
  ┌────────┐              ┌────────┐
5 │        │      6       │        │
  │        │ + 2 ┌──────┐ + 5 │        │
  └────────┘     └──────┘     └────────┘
```

The length of the middle rectangle (above) is $5 - \boxed{} = \boxed{}$.

$A = (6 \cdot \boxed{}) + (6 \cdot \boxed{}) + (6 \cdot \boxed{})$ Add the areas together.

$= \boxed{} + \boxed{} + \boxed{}$

$= \boxed{}$ square units

Holt Mathematics

Check It Out!

1. Find the perimeter of the parallelogram.

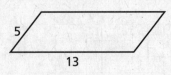

2. Graph and find the area of the figure with the given vertices.
   (−3, −2), (1, −2), (1, 3), (−3, 3)

3. Find the perimeter of the figure.

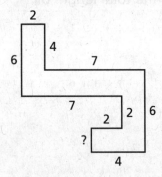

Perimeter and Area of Triangles and Trapezoids

Lesson Objectives

Find the perimeter and area of triangles and trapezoids

Additional Examples

Example 1

Find the missing measurement for the trapezoid with perimeter 71 in.

18 in.
15 in.
22 in.

$P = \boxed{} + \boxed{} + \boxed{} + d$

$71 = \boxed{} + d$ Substitute $\boxed{}$ for P.

$-55 \quad -55$ Subtract $\boxed{}$ from both sides.

$16 = \qquad d$

$d = \boxed{}$

Example 2

A homeowner wants to plant a border of shrubs around her yard that is in the shape of a right triangle. She knows that the length of the shortest side of the yard is 12 feet and the length of the longest side is 20 feet. How long will the border be?

A. Find the length of the third side.

$a^2 + b^2 = c^2$ Use the Pythagorean Theorem.

$\boxed{}^2 + b^2 = \boxed{}^2$ Substitute $\boxed{}$ for a and $\boxed{}$ for c.

$\boxed{} + b^2 = \boxed{}$

$b^2 = \boxed{}$

$b = \boxed{}$ $\sqrt{256} = \boxed{}$

Holt Mathematics

B. Find the perimeter of the yard.

$P = a + b + c$

$= \boxed{} + \boxed{} + \boxed{}$ *Add all sides.*

$= \boxed{}$

The border will be $\boxed{}$ feet long.

Example 3

Graph and find the area of the figure with the given vertices.

(–2, 2), (4, 2), (0,5)

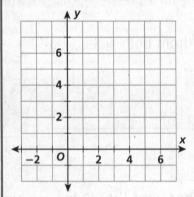

The base of the triangle is $\boxed{}$ units, and the height of the triangle is

$\boxed{}$ units.

$A = \frac{1}{2}bh$ Area of triangle

$A = \frac{1}{2} \cdot \boxed{} \cdot \boxed{}$ Substitute for *b* and *h*.

$A = \boxed{}$ units

Holt Mathematics

Check It Out!

1. Find the missing measurement when the perimeter is 58 in.

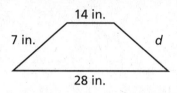

14 in.

7 in.

d

28 in.

2. A gardener wants to plant a border of flowers around the building that is in the shape of a right triangle. He knows that the lengths of the shortest sides of the building are 38 feet and 32 feet. How long will the border be?

3. Graph and find the area of the figure with the given vertices. (−1, −2), (5, −2), (5, 2), (−1, 6)

Holt Mathematics

LESSON 9-3 **Circles**

Lesson Objectives

Identify parts of a circle and find central angle measures

Vocabulary

circle (p. 446) _____

_____

center of a circle (p. 446) _____

_____

arc (p. 446) _____

radius (p. 446) _____

_____

diameter (p. 446) _____

_____

chord (p. 446) _____

central angle (p. 447) _____

sector (p. 447) _____

_____

Additional Examples

Example 1

Name the parts of circle M.

A. radii

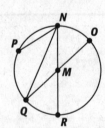

B. diameters

C. chords

Holt Mathematics

Example 2

PROBLEM SOLVING APPLICATION

The circle graph shows the results of a survey about favorite types of muffins. Find the central angle measure of the sector that shows the percent of people whose favorite type of muffin is blueberry.

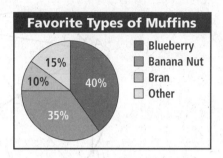

Favorite Types of Muffins

- ■ Blueberry
- ■ Banana Nut
- ▨ Bran
- ☐ Other

15%
10%
40%
35%

1. **Understand the Problem**

   The answer is the measure of the central angle that represents blueberry. List the important information:

   - The percent of people whose favorite muffin is blueberry is ☐ %.

   - The central angle measure of the sector that represents this group is

     ☐ % of the ☐° of the circle.

2. **Make a Plan**

   There are ☐° in a circle. Since the sector is 40% of the circle graph,

   the central angle is ☐ % of the 360° in the circle.

   ☐ % of 360° = 0.40 · 360°

3. **Solve**

   0.40 · 360° = ☐°   Multiply.

   The central angle of the sector is ☐° .

4. **Look Back**

   The 40% sector is less than half the graph, and 144° is less than half of 360°. Therefore, the answer is reasonable.

Holt Mathematics

Check It Out!

1. Name the radii, diameters, and chords of circle *M*.

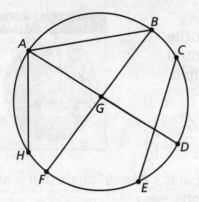

2. The circle graph shows the results of a survey about favorite types of muffins. Find the central angle measure of the sector that shows the percent of people whose favorite type of muffin is banana nut.

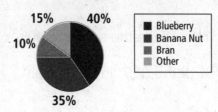

Favorite Types of Muffins

LESSON 9-4 **Circumference and Area**

Lesson Objectives

Find the circumference and area of circles

Vocabulary

circumference (p. 450) _____

Additional Examples

Example 1

Find the circumference of each circle, both in terms of π and to the nearest tenth. Use 3.14 for π.

A. circle with a radius of 4 m

$C = 2\pi r$

$= 2\pi(\boxed{})$

$= \boxed{}\,\pi$ m $\approx \boxed{}$ m

B. circle with a diameter of 3.3 ft

$C = \pi d$

$= \pi(\boxed{})$

$= \boxed{}\,\pi$ ft $\approx \boxed{}$ ft

Example 2

Find the area of each circle, both in terms of π and to the nearest tenth. Use 3.14 for π.

A. circle with a radius of 4 in.

$A = \pi r^2 = \pi(\boxed{})^2$

$= \boxed{}\,\pi$ in² $\approx \boxed{}$ in²

B. circle with a diameter of 3.3 m

$A = \pi r^2 = \pi(\boxed{})^2 \qquad \dfrac{d}{2} = \boxed{}$

$= \boxed{}\,\pi$ m² $\approx \boxed{}$ m²

Holt Mathematics

Example 3

Graph the circle with center (−2, 1) that passes through (1, 1). Find the area and circumference, both in terms of π and to the nearest tenth. Use 3.14 for π.

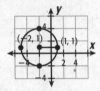

$A = \pi r^2$

$= \pi(\boxed{})^2$

$= \boxed{}\,\pi$ units^2

$\approx \boxed{}$ units^2

$C = \pi d$

$= \pi(\boxed{})$

$= \boxed{}\,\pi$ units

$\approx \boxed{}$ units

Example 4

A. Ferris wheel has a diameter of 56 feet and makes 15 revolutions per ride. How far would someone travel during a ride? Use $\frac{22}{7}$ for π.

$C = \pi d = \pi(\boxed{})$ Find the circumference.

$\approx \frac{22}{7}\left(\dfrac{\boxed{}}{1}\right) = \boxed{}$

The distance traveled is the circumference of the Ferris wheel times the

number of revolutions, or about $\boxed{} \cdot \boxed{} \approx \boxed{}$ ft.

Check It Out!

1. Find the circumference of the circle, both in terms of π and to the nearest tenth. Use 3.14 for π.

circle with a diameter of 4.25 in.

Holt Mathematics

2. **Find the area of the circle, both in terms of π and to the nearest tenth. Use 3.14 for π.**

   circle with a radius of 8 cm

3. **Graph the circle with center (–2, 1) that passes through (–2, 5). Find the area and circumference, both in terms of π and to the nearest tenth. Use 3.14 for π.**

4. **A second hand on a clock is 7 in long. What is the distance it travels in one hour? Use $\frac{22}{7}$ for π.**

Holt Mathematics

LESSON 9-5

Area of Composite Figures

Lesson Objectives

Find the area of composite figures

Additional Examples

Example 1

Find the shaded area. Round to the nearest tenth, if necessary.

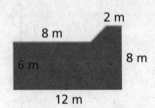

2 m

8 m

8 m

6 m

12 m

Divide the figure into a rectangle and a trapezoid.

Area of the rectangle:

$A = bh$

$A = \boxed{} \cdot \boxed{}$ Substitute $\boxed{}$ for b and $\boxed{}$ for h

$A = \boxed{}$ m²

Area of the trapezoid:

$A = \frac{1}{2}h(b_1 + b_2)$

$A = \frac{1}{2}\boxed{}(\boxed{} + \boxed{})$ Substitute $\boxed{}$ for h, $\boxed{}$ for b_1, and $\boxed{}$ for b_2.

$A = \frac{1}{2}(\boxed{})$ Simplify.

$A = \boxed{}$ m²

Add the area of the rectangle and the area of the trapezoid.

Total area: $A = \boxed{} + \boxed{} = \boxed{}$ m²

Holt Mathematics

Example 2

Find the shaded area.

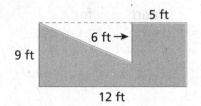

9 ft

5 ft

6 ft →

12 ft

Subtract the area of the triangle from the area of the rectangle.

Area of the rectangle:

$A = bh$

$A = \boxed{} \cdot \boxed{} = \boxed{}$ ft²   Substitute $\boxed{}$ for b and $\boxed{}$ for h.

Area of the triangle:

$A = \frac{1}{2}(bh)$

$A = \frac{1}{2}(\boxed{})(\boxed{})$ Substitute $\boxed{}$ for b and $\boxed{}$ for h.

$A = \frac{1}{2}(\boxed{}) = \boxed{}$ ft²   Simplify.

Shaded area: $A = \boxed{} - \boxed{} = \boxed{}$ ft²

Example 3

What is the area of the room floor shown in the figure? Round to the nearest tenth.

To find the area, divide the composite figure into a square, a rectangle, and a semicircle.

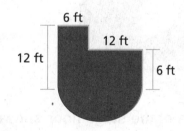

6 ft

12 ft

12 ft

6 ft

Area of the square:

$A = s^2$

$A = \boxed{}^2 = \boxed{}$ ft²

$A = \boxed{}$ ft²

Area of the rectangle:

$A = bh$

$A = \boxed{} \cdot \boxed{}$

$A = \boxed{}$ ft²

Holt Mathematics

Area of the semicircle:

$A = \frac{1}{2}\pi r^2$

$A = \frac{1}{2}\left(\boxed{} \cdot \boxed{}^2 \right)$ Substitute 3.14 for $\boxed{}$ and $\boxed{}$ for r.

$A = \frac{1}{2}\left(\boxed{} \right)$ Simplify.

$A = \boxed{}$

Area of the room: $A = \boxed{} + \boxed{} + \boxed{} =$

$\boxed{}$, or approximately $\boxed{}$ ft².

Check It Out!

1. Find the shaded area. Round to the nearest tenth, if necessary.

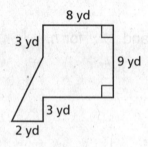

8 yd

3 yd

9 yd

3 yd

2 yd

2. Find the shaded area.

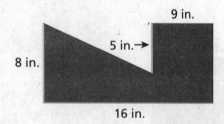

9 in.

5 in.→

8 in.

16 in.

3. What is the area of the stage floor shown in the figure? Round to the nearest tenth.

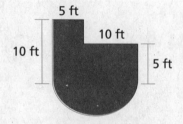

5 ft

10 ft

10 ft

5 ft

Holt Mathematics

California Standards MG2.2

Area of Irregular Figures

LESSON 9-6

Lesson Objectives

Estimate the area of irregular figures

Additional Examples

Example 1

A. Find the area of the figure.

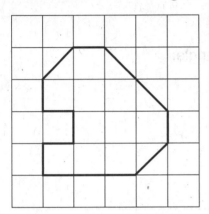

Count the full squares: ☐

Count the half-squares: ☐

Add the number of full squares plus half the number of half-full squares:

☐ + ($\frac{1}{2}$ · ☐) = ☐ + ☐ = ☐

The area of the figure is ☐ square units.

B. Find the area of the figure.

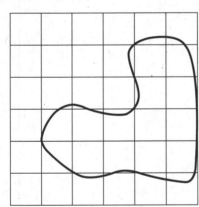

Count the full and almost-full squares: ☐

Count the half-full squares: ☐

Add the number of full squares plus half the number of half-full squares:

☐ + ($\frac{1}{2}$ · ☐) = ☐ + ☐ = ☐

The area of the figure is approximately

☐ square units.

Holt Mathematics

Example 2

Use a composite figure to estimate the shaded area.

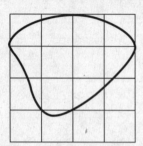

Draw a composite figure that approximates the irregular shape. Divide the composite figure into simple shapes, like a trapezoid and a triangle.

Area of the trapezoid:

$$A = \frac{1}{2}h(b_1 + b_2)$$

$$A = \frac{1}{2}(\boxed{})(\boxed{} + \boxed{}) = \boxed{}$$

Area of the triangle:

$$A = \frac{1}{2}(bh)$$

$$A = \frac{1}{2}(\boxed{} \cdot \boxed{}) = \boxed{}$$

The area is approximately $\boxed{}$ square units.

Check It Out!

Find the area of each figure.

1.

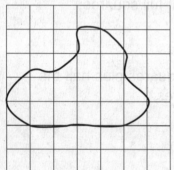

2.

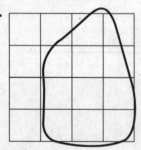

Holt Mathematics

CHAPTER 9

Chapter Review

9-1 Perimeter and Area of Parallelograms

Find the perimeter and area of each figure.

1.

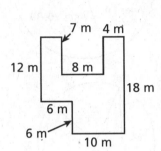

2.

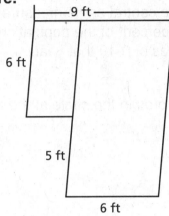

3. The dance floor at a graduation dinner reception is a rectangular shape with dimensions 16 ft by 28 ft. What is the area of the dance floor?

9-2 Perimeter and Area of Triangles and Trapezoids

Find the area of each figure with the given dimensions.

4. triangle: $b = 9$, $h = 15$

5. trapezoid: $b_1 = 7$, $b_2 = 12$, $h = 5$

Find the perimeter of each figure.

6.

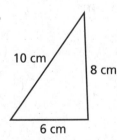

7.

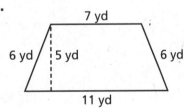

8.

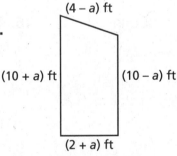

9. The perimeter of a triangle is 46.9 ft. Two of its sides measure 14.8 ft and 21.2 ft, respectively. What is the length of its third side of the triangle?

Holt Mathematics

9-3 Circles

10. The circle graph shows the population of the United States in 2005, according to the U.S. Census Bureau. Find the central angle measure of the sector that shows the percent of the population that was between the ages of 0-19 that year.

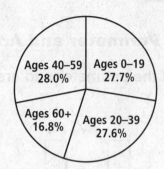

11. Name all the chords in the circle at the right.

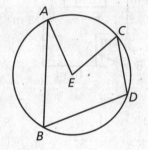

9-4 Circumference and Area

Find the circumference and area of each circle to the nearest tenth. Use 3.14 for π.

12.

3.4 m

13.

18 ft

14.

7 in.

Find the radius of each circle with the given measurement.

15. $C = 85\pi$ in.

16. $A = 256\pi$ cm^2

17. $A = 179.56\pi$ m^2

Holt Mathematics

9-5 Area of Composite Figures

Find the area. Use 3.14 for π and round to the nearest tenth, if necessary.

18.

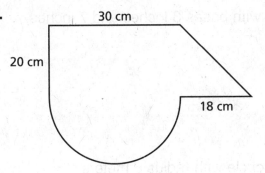

30 cm

20 cm

18 cm

19.

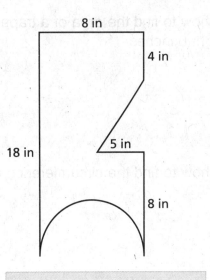

8 in

4 in

18 in

5 in

8 in

9-6 Area of Irregular Figures

Find the area of each figure.

20.

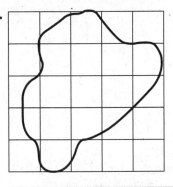

21.

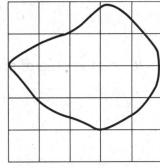

Holt Mathematics

Big Ideas

Answer these questions to summarize the important concepts from Chapter 9 in your own words.

1. Explain how to find the area of a trapezoid with bases 3 inches and 7 inches, and height 6 inches.

2. Explain how to find the circumference of a circle with radius 6 meters.

3. Explain two ways to find the area of a composite figure.

4. Explain two ways to find the area of an irregular figure.

For more review of Chapter 9:

- Complete the Chapter 9 Study Guide and Review on pages 466–468 of your textbook.

- Complete the Ready to Go On quizzes on pages 444 and 462 of your textbook.

Holt Mathematics

Three-Dimensional Figures

Lesson Objectives

Identify various three-dimensional figures

Vocabulary

face (p. 480) _____

_____

edge (p. 480) _____

_____

polyhedron (p. 480) _____

_____

vertex (p. 480) _____

_____

base (p. 480) _____

_____

prism (p. 480) _____

_____

pyramid (p. 480) _____

_____

cylinder (p. 481) _____

_____

cone (p. 481) _____

_____

Holt Mathematics

Additional Examples

Example 1

Identify the base or bases of the solid. Then name the solid.

A.

There is one base, and it is a [   ].

There are [   ] triangular faces.

The figure is a [   ].

B.

There is one base, and it is a [   ].

There are [   ] triangular faces.

The figure is a [   ].

C.

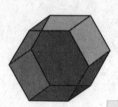

There are two bases, and they are [   ]

There are [   ] rectangular faces.

The figure is a [   ].

Holt Mathematics

Example 2

Classify each figure as a polyhedron or not a polyhedron. Then name the figure.

A.

The faces are all [_____], so the

figure [_____] a polyhedron.

There is one [_____] base for

each figure.

The figure is made up of a rectangular [_____] and a

rectangular [_____].

B.

The [_____] are not all polygons, so the figure

[_____] a polyhedron.

There is one [_____] base.

The figure is a [_____].

C.

The faces are not all [_____], so the

figure [_____] a polyhedron.

There are two [_____] bases.

The figure is a [_____].

Holt Mathematics

Check It Out!

1. Describe the bases and faces of the figure. Then name the figure.

2. Classify each figure as a polyhedron or not a polyhedron. Then name the figure.

Holt Mathematics

LESSON 10-2

Volume of Prisms and Cylinders

Know it! Note

Lesson Objectives

Find the volume of prisms and cylinders

Vocabulary

volume (p. 485) _____

_____

Additional Examples

Example 1

Find the volume of each figure to the nearest tenth. Use 3.14 for π.

A.

12 in.

Cereal

2 in.

8 in.

$B = \boxed{} \cdot \boxed{} = \boxed{}$ in²   The base is a $\boxed{}$.

$V = Bh$ $\boxed{}$ of a prism.

$= \boxed{} \cdot \boxed{}$ Substitute for $\boxed{}$ and $\boxed{}$.

$= \boxed{}$ in³   Multiply.

B.

4 in.

12 in.

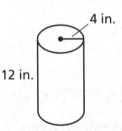

$B = \pi(\boxed{})^2 = \boxed{} \pi$ in²   The base is a $\boxed{}$.

$V = Bh$ Volume of a $\boxed{}$

$= \boxed{} \pi \cdot \boxed{}$ Substitute for B and h.

$= \boxed{} \pi \approx \boxed{}$ in³   Multiply.

Holt Mathematics

C.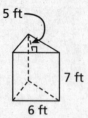

5 ft

7 ft

6 ft

$B =$ ☐ · ☐ · ☐ = ☐ ft² The base is a ☐ .

$V = Bh$ Volume of a ☐

   = ☐ · ☐   Substitute for B and h.

   = ☐ ft³   Multiply.

Example 2

A. A juice box measures 3 in. by 2 in. by 4 in. Explain whether tripling the length, width, or height of the box would triple the amount of juice the box holds.

Original Dimensions	Triple the Length	Triple the Width	Triple the Height
$V = lwh$	$V = (3l)wh$	$V = l(3w)h$	$V = lw(3h)$
= ☐ · ☐ · ☐	= ☐ · 2 · 4	= 3 · ☐ · 4	= 3 · 2 · ☐
= ☐ in³	= ☐ in³	= ☐ in³	= ☐ in³

The original box has a volume of ☐ in³. You could triple the volume to

☐ in³ by tripling any one of the dimensions. So tripling the length, width,

or height ☐ triple the amount of juice the box holds.

Holt Mathematics

B. A juice can has a radius of 2 in. and a height of 5 in. Explain whether tripling only the height of the can would have the same effect on the volume as tripling the radius.

Original Dimensions	Triple the Radius	Triple the Height
$V = \pi r^2 h$	$V = \pi (3r)^2 h$	$V = \pi r^2 (3h)$
$= \boxed{}^2 \pi \cdot \boxed{}$	$= \boxed{}^2 \pi \cdot \boxed{}$	$= \boxed{}^2 \pi \cdot \boxed{}$
$= \boxed{} \pi$ in^3	$= \boxed{} \pi$ in^3	$= \boxed{} \pi$ in^3

By tripling the height, you would $\boxed{}$ the volume. By tripling the radius, you would increase the volume to $\boxed{}$ times the original volume.

Example 3

A drum company advertises a snare drum that is 4 inches high and 12 inches in diameter. Estimate the volume of the drum.

$$r = \frac{d}{2} = \frac{\boxed{}}{2} = \boxed{}$$

$$V = (\pi r^2)h \qquad\qquad \text{Volume of a } \boxed{}$$

$$= (3.14)(\boxed{})^2 (\boxed{}) \qquad \text{Use } \boxed{} \text{ for } \pi.$$

$$= (3.14)(\boxed{})(4)$$

$$= \boxed{} \cdot 4$$

$$= \boxed{} \approx \boxed{} \text{ in}^3$$

Holt Mathematics

Example 4

Find the volume of the barn.

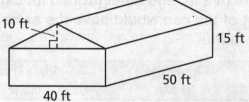

Volume of barn	=	Volume of rectangular prism	+	Volume of triangular prism

$$V = (40)(50)(15) \qquad + \frac{1}{2}(40)(10)(50)$$

$$= \boxed{} \qquad + \boxed{}$$

$$= \boxed{} \text{ ft}^3$$

The volume is _____ ft³.

Check It Out!

1. Find the volume of the figure to the nearest tenth.

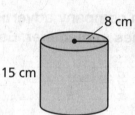

2. A box measures 5 in. by 3 in. by 7 in.
   Explain whether tripling only the length, width, or height
   of the box would triple the volume of the box.

3. A drum company advertises a bass drum that is 12 inches high and
   28 inches in diameter. Estimate the volume of the drum.

4. Find the volume of the play house.

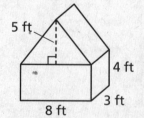

Holt Mathematics

LESSON 10-3

Volume of Pyramids and Cones

Know it!
.Note

Lesson Objectives

Find the volume of pyramids and cones

Additional Examples

Example 1

Find the volume of each figure. Use 3.14 for π.

A.

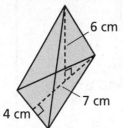

6 cm

7 cm

4 cm

$B = \frac{1}{2}(\boxed{} \cdot \boxed{}) = \boxed{}$ cm²

$V = \frac{1}{3} \cdot \boxed{} \cdot \boxed{}$ $V = \frac{1}{3}Bh$

$V = \boxed{}$ cm³

B.

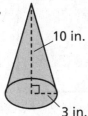

10 in.

3 in.

$B = \pi(\boxed{})^2 = \boxed{}\pi$ in²

$V = \frac{1}{3} \cdot \boxed{}\pi \cdot \boxed{}$ $V = \frac{1}{3}Bh$

$V = \boxed{}\pi \approx \boxed{}$ in³   Use 3.14 for $\boxed{}$.

Example 2

The Pyramid of Kukulcán in Mexico is a square pyramid. Its height is 24 m and its base has 55 m sides. Find the volume of the pyramid.

Step 1 Find the area of the base.

$B = \boxed{}^2 = \boxed{}$ m² $A = bh$

Step 2 Find the volume.

$V = \frac{1}{3}(\boxed{})(\boxed{})$ $V = \frac{1}{3}bh$

$V = \boxed{}$ m³

Holt Mathematics

Check It Out!

1. Find the volume of the figure. Use 3.14 for π.

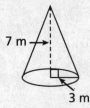

7 m

3 m

2. Find the volume of a square pyramid with a height of 12 m and a base with 48 m sides.

238
Holt Mathematics

LESSON 10-4 **Surface Area of Prisms and Cylinders**

Lesson Objectives

Find the surface area of prisms and cylinders

Vocabulary

surface area (p. 498) _____

_____

lateral face (p. 498) _____

_____

lateral area (p. 498) _____

_____

lateral surface (p. 499) _____

_____

Additional Examples

Example 1

Find the surface area of each figure. The figure is made up of congruent cubes.

A.

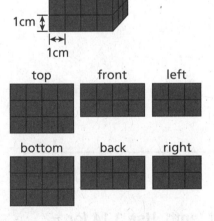

top   front   left

bottom   back   right

Draw each view of the figure.

Find the area of each view.

The surface area is [ ] cm².

Holt Mathematics

B.

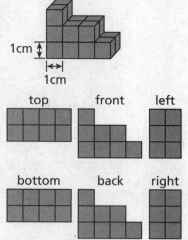

1cm
1cm

| top | front | left |
| bottom | back | right |

Draw each view of the figure.

Find the area of each view.

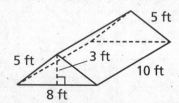

□ + □ + □ + □ + □ + □ = □

The surface area is ▭ cm².

Example 2

Find the surface area of the prism to the nearest tenth.

5 ft

5 ft   3 ft

8 ft   10 ft

$S = 2B + P = 2(\square \cdot \square \cdot \square) + (\square)(\square)$

$= \square$ ft²

Example 3

Find the surface area of the cylinder to the nearest tenth. Use 3.14 for π.

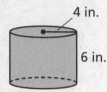

4 in.

6 in.

$S = 2\pi r^2 + 2\pi rh$

$= 2\pi(\square^2) + 2\pi(\square)(\square)$

$= \square \pi$ in² $\approx$ ▭ in²

Holt Mathematics

Example 4

A cylindrical soup can is 7.6 cm in diameter and 11.2 cm tall. Estimate the area of the label that covers the side of the can.

$L = 2\pi rh$ Only the lateral surface needs to be covered.

$= 2\pi(\boxed{})(\boxed{})$ diameter $\approx$ 8 cm, so $r \approx \boxed{}$ cm.

$= \boxed{}\,\pi \approx \boxed{}$ cm³

Check It Out!

1. Find the area of the figure. The figure is made up of congruent cubes.

2. Find the surface area of the figure to the nearest tenth.

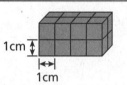

3. Find the surface area of the figure.

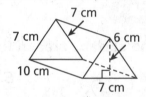

4. A cylindrical storage tank that is 6 ft in diameter and 12 ft tall needs to be painted. Estimate the area to be painted.

Holt Mathematics

California Standards Ext. of MG2.1

Surface Area of Pyramids and Cones

Lesson Objectives

Find the surface area of pyramids and cones

Vocabulary

slant height (p. 504) _____

_____

regular pyramid (p. 504) _____

_____

right cone (p. 504) _____

_____

Additional Examples

Example 1

Find the surface area of the figure to the nearest tenth.

A.

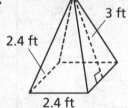

3 ft

2.4 ft

2.4 ft

$S = B + \frac{1}{2}Pl$

$= (\boxed{} \cdot \boxed{}) + \frac{1}{2}(\boxed{})(\boxed{})$

$= \boxed{}$ ft^2

Holt Mathematics

Example 2

A cone has diameter 8 in. and slant height 3 in. Explain whether tripling the slant height would have the same effect on the surface area as tripling the radius.

Original Dimensions	Triple the Slant Height	Triple the Radius
$S = \pi r^2 + \pi r l$	$S = \pi r^2 + \pi r(3l)$	$S = \pi (3r)^2 + \pi (3r)l$
$= \pi(4)^2 + \pi(4)(3)$	$= \pi(4)^2 + \pi(4)(9)$	$= \pi(12)^2 + \pi(12)(3)$
$= 28\pi$ in$^2 \approx$ ⬚	$= 52\pi$ in$^2 \approx$ ⬚	$= 180\pi$ in$^2 \approx$ ⬚

They ⬚ have the same effect. Tripling the radius would

increase the surface area ⬚ than tripling the slant height.

Example 3

The upper portion of an hourglass is approximately an inverted cone with the given dimensions. What is the lateral surface area of the upper portion of the hourglass?

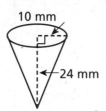

10 mm

24 mm

$$a^2 + b^2 = l^2 \qquad \text{Pythagorean Theorem}$$

$$\boxed{}^2 + \boxed{}^2 = l^2$$

$$\boxed{} = l^2$$

$$l = \boxed{}$$

$$L = \pi r l \qquad \text{Lateral surface area}$$

$$= \pi(\boxed{})(\boxed{}) = \boxed{}\,\pi \approx \boxed{} \text{ mm}^2$$

Holt Mathematics

LESSON 10-5 *CONTINUED*

Check It Out!

1. Find the surface area of the figure to the nearest tenth.
   Use 3.14 for π.

2. A cone has diameter 9 in. and a slant height 2 in. Explain whether tripling only the slant height would have the same effect on the surface area as tripling only the radius. Use the 3.14 for π.

3. A large road construction cone is almost a full cone. With the given dimensions, what is the lateral surface area of the cone?

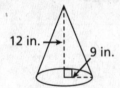

Holt Mathematics

LESSON 10-6 **Spheres**

Lesson Objectives

Find the volume and surface area of spheres

Vocabulary

sphere (p. 436) _____

_____

hemisphere (p. 436) _____

_____

Additional Examples

Example 1

Find the volume of a sphere with radius 12 cm, both in terms of π and to the nearest tenth of a unit. Use 3.14 for π.

$V = \left(\frac{4}{3}\right)\pi r^3$ 　　 [_____] of a sphere

$= \left(\frac{4}{3}\right)\pi \left([\quad]\right)^3$ 　Substitute [___] for r.

$= [\qquad] \pi \text{ cm}^3 \approx [\qquad] \text{ cm}^3$

Example 2

Find the surface area, both in terms of π and to the nearest tenth of a unit. Use 3.14 for π.

$S = 4\pi r^2$ 　　 [_____] area of a sphere

$= 4\pi \left([\quad]\right)^2$ 　Substitute [___] for r.

$= [\qquad] \pi \text{ in}^2 \approx [\qquad] \text{ in}^2$

3 in.

Holt Mathematics

Example 3

Compare the volume and surface area of a sphere with radius 42 cm with that of a rectangular prism measuring 44 cm by 84 cm by 84 cm.

Sphere:

$V = \left(\frac{4}{3}\right)\pi r^3 = \left(\frac{4}{3}\right)\pi(\boxed{})^3$

$\approx \left(\frac{4}{3}\right)\left(\frac{22}{7}\right)\boxed{}$

$\approx \boxed{}$ cm³

$S = 4\pi r^2 = 4\pi(\boxed{})^2$

$= \boxed{}\ \pi$

$\approx \boxed{}\left(\frac{22}{7}\right)$

$\approx \boxed{}$ cm²

Rectangular Prism:

$V = lwh$

$= (\boxed{})(\boxed{})(\boxed{})$

$= \boxed{}$ cm³

$S = 2lw + 2lh + 2wh$

$= 2(\boxed{})(\boxed{}) +$

$\quad 2(\boxed{})(\boxed{}) +$

$\quad 2(\boxed{})(\boxed{})$

$= \boxed{}$ cm²

The sphere and the prism have approximately the same \boxed{},

but the prism has a \boxed{} surface area.

Holt Mathematics

Check It Out!

1. Find the volume of a sphere with radius 3 cm, both in terms of π and to the nearest tenth of a unit.

2. The moon has a radius of 1,738 km. Find the surface area, both in terms of π and to the nearest tenth.

3. Compare the volume and surface area of a sphere with radius 21 mm with that of a rectangular prism measuring 22 mm by 42 mm by 42 mm.

Holt Mathematics

LESSON 10-7 Scaling Three-Dimensional Figures

Lesson Objectives

Find the volume and surface area of similar three-dimensional figures

Additional Examples

Example 1

A 3 cm cube is built from small cubes, each 1 cm on an edge. Compare the following values.

A. the edge lengths of the large and small cubes

$\dfrac{3 \text{ cm cube}}{1 \text{ cm cube}} \rightarrow \dfrac{\boxed{} \text{ cm}}{\boxed{} \text{ cm}} = \boxed{}$ Ratio of corresponding $\boxed{}$.

The edges of the large cube are $\boxed{}$ times as long as the edges of the small cube.

B. the surface areas of the two cubes

$\dfrac{3 \text{ cm cube}}{1 \text{ cm cube}} \rightarrow \dfrac{\boxed{} \text{ cm}^2}{\boxed{} \text{ cm}^2} = \boxed{}$ Ratio of corresponding $\boxed{}$.

The surface area of the larger cube is $\boxed{}$ times that of the smaller cube.

C. the volumes of the two cubes

$\dfrac{3 \text{ cm cube}}{1 \text{ cm cube}} \rightarrow \dfrac{\boxed{} \text{ cm}^2}{\boxed{} \text{ cm}^2} = \boxed{}$ Ratio of corresponding $\boxed{}$.

The volume of the larger cube is $\boxed{}$ times that of the smaller cube.

Holt Mathematics

Example 2

A. The surface area of a box is 1300 in². What is the surface area of a similar box that is smaller by a scale factor of $\frac{1}{2}$?

$S = \boxed{} \cdot (\boxed{})^2$ Multiply by the $\boxed{}$ of the scale factor.

$= \boxed{} \cdot \boxed{}$ Simplify the power.

$= \boxed{}$ in²   Multiply.

B. The volume of a child's swimming pool is 28 ft³. What is the volume of a similar pool that is larger by a scale factor of 4?

$V = \boxed{} \cdot \boxed{}^3$ Multiply by the $\boxed{}$ of the scale factor.

$= \boxed{} \cdot \boxed{}$ Simplify the power.

$= \boxed{}$ ft³   Multiply.

Example 3

It takes 30 seconds for a pump to fill a cubic container whose edge measures 1 ft. How long does it take for the pump to fill a cubic container whose edge measures 2 ft?

$V = \boxed{}$ ft $\cdot \boxed{}$ ft $\cdot \boxed{}$ ft $= \boxed{}$ ft³   Find the volume of the larger container.

Set up a proportion and solve.

$\dfrac{30}{1\ \text{ft}^3} = \dfrac{x}{\boxed{}\ \text{ft}^3}$ Cancel units.

$\boxed{} \cdot \boxed{} = \boxed{}$ Multiply.

$\boxed{} = x$ Calculate the fill time.

It takes $\boxed{}$ seconds, or $\boxed{}$ minutes to fill the larger container.

Holt Mathematics

Check It Out!

1. A 2 cm cube is built from small cubes, each 1 cm on an edge. Compare the following values.

   the edge lengths of the large and small cubes

2. The volume of a small hot tub is 48 ft³. What is the volume of a similar hot tub that is larger by a scale factor of 2?

3. It takes 30 seconds for a pump to fill a cubic container whose edge measures 1 ft. How long does it take for the pump to fill a cubic container whose edge measures 3 ft?

Holt Mathematics

Chapter Review

10-1 Three-Dimensional Figures

Classify each figure as a polyhedron or not a polyhedron. Then name the figure.

1.
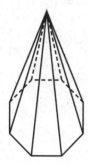

2.
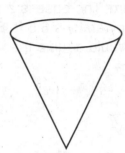

3.
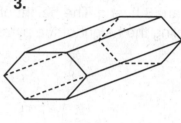

Classify each figure as a polyhedron or not a polyhedron. Then name the figure.

4. one rectangular base and four triangular faces

5. two parallel, congruent triangular bases and three other polygonal faces

10-2 Volume of Prisms and Cylinders

Find the volume of each figure to the nearest tenth.

6.
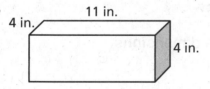

7.
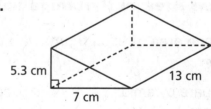

8. A can of soup has a radius 3.5 in. and a height 8 in. Explain whether increasing the radius 4 times would increase the volume by 4 times.

Holt Mathematics

10-3 Volume of Pyramids and Cones

9. Kerri made cone-shaped containers. The diameter of the container is 7 in. and the height is 11 in. What is the volume of the container to the nearest tenth?

10. Hector built a pyramid in his backyard. The base is a square, with sides that are 8 ft long. The height of the pyramid is 6.5 ft. Explain whether doubling the height of the pyramid would double the volume of the pyramid.

10-4 Surface Area of Prisms and Cylinders

Find the surface area of each figure with the given dimensions to the nearest tenth. Use 3.14 for π.

11.

9 cm

24 cm

12.

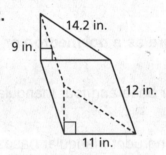

14.2 in.

9 in.

12 in.

11 in.

13. Jillian wants to make a box that is 6 in. by 6 in. by 22 in. How many square inches of cardboard does she need?

10-5 Surface Area of Pyramids and Cones

Find the surface area of each figure with the given dimensions. Use 3.14 for π.

14. regular square pyramid:
base perimeter = 60 yd
slant height = 6 yd

15. cone:
radius = 18.4 m
slant height = 32 m

Holt Mathematics

10-6 Spheres

Find the missing measurements of each sphere, both in terms of π and to the nearest tenth. Use 3.14 for π.

16. radius = 8.6 in.
volume = ?
surface area = ?

17. diameter = 4.6 mm
volume = ?
surface area = ?

10-7 Scaling Three-Dimensional Figures

A 10 cm cube is built from small cubes, each 2 cm on a side. Compare the following values.

18. the surface area of the two cubes   **19.** the volumes of the two cubes

20. A bath tub measures 60 in. by 30 in. by 18 in. It takes 54 minutes to fill with water. A larger bath tub measures 68 in. by 36 in. by 20 in. About how long will it take to fill the larger bath tub with water?

Holt Mathematics

Big Ideas

Answer these questions to summarize the important concepts from Chapter 10 in your own words.

1. Explain why cylinders and cones are not polyhedrons.

2. Explain how to find the volume of a cone with radius 3 feet and height 8 feet.

3. Explain how to find the surface area of a cylinder with diameter 6 inches and height 7 inches.

4. The surface area of a box is 34 cm². Explain how to find the surface area of a similar box that is larger by a scale factor of 9.

For more review of Chapter 10:

- Complete the Chapter 10 Study Guide: Review on pages 520–522 of your textbook.

- Complete the Ready to Go On quizzes on pages 494 and 516 of your textbook.

Holt Mathematics

California Standards SDAP1.1

LESSON 11-1 Line Plots and Stem-and-Leaf Plots

Lesson Objectives

Organize and interpret data in line plots and stem-and-leaf plots

Vocabulary

line plot (p. 532) _____

_____

stem-and-leaf plot (p. 533) _____

_____

back-to-back stem-and-leaf plot (p. 533) _____

_____

_____

Additional Examples

Example 1

Use a line plot to organize the math exam scores.

Student Test Scores			
100	95	75	80
60	100	60	75
90	85	80	100
50	90	65	80

Find the least value, ☐, and the greatest value, ☐, in the data

set. Then draw a number line from ☐ to ☐. Place an "*x*" above
each number on the number line for each time it appears in the data set.

```
                    x       x
        x       x   x   x   x
    x   x   x   x   x   x   x   x
    +---+---+---+---+---+---+---+---+---+---+
    50 55 60 65 70 75 80 85 90 95 100
```

There are ☐ numbers in the data set

and ☐ *x*'s above the number line.

Holt Mathematics

Example 2

The data shows the number of years coached by the top 15 leaders in all-time NFL coaching victories. Make a stem-and-leaf plot of the data. Then find the number of coaches who coached fewer than 25 years.

33, 40, 29, 33, 23, 22, 20, 21, 18, 23, 17, 15, 15, 12, 17

Step 1: Find the least data value and the greatest data value.

Since the data values range from [ ] to [ ], use tens digits

for the [ ] and ones digits for the [ ].

Step 2: List the [ ] from least to greatest on the plot.

Step 3: List the [ ] for each stem from least to greatest.

Step 4: Add a [ ] and a [ ]. The stems are the

[ ] digits. The leaves are the [ ] digits.

[ ] coaches coached fewer than 25 years.

Example 3

Use the given data to make a back-to-back stem-and-leaf plot.

U.S. Representatives for Selected States, 1950 and 2000					
	IL	MA	MI	NY	PA
1950	25	14	18	43	31
2000	19	10	15	29	19

Holt Mathematics

Check It Out!

1. Use a line plot to organize the feet of snow each season.

Feet of Snow			
4	11	7	5
1	9	5	10
7	4	3	9
11	10	7	6
5	9	9	11

2. The list shows the number of times each soccer player can bounce the ball on their knee. How many soccer players can bounce the ball more than 36 times?

55, 60, 33, 30, 23, 45, 28, 41, 62, 29, 35, 40, 43, 37, 68, 30, 61, 27, 38, 41

3. Use the given data to make a back-to-back stem-and-leaf plot.

Voting Statistics		
Age	Voted	Did Not Vote
	Millions	Millions
18 to 24 years	8	18
25 to 34 years	16	21
35 to 44 years	24	20
45 to 54 years	23	14
55 to 64 years	16	8
65 to 74 years	12	5
75 years up	10	5

Holt Mathematics

Mean, Medium, Mode, and Range
LESSON 11-2

Lesson Objectives

Find the mean, median, mode, and range of a data set

Vocabulary

mean (p. 537) _____

_____

median (p. 537) _____

mode (p. 537) _____

range (p. 537) _____

_____

outlier (p. 538) _____

_____

Holt Mathematics

Additional Examples

Example 1

Find the mean, median, mode, and range of the data set.

4, 7, 8, 2, 1, 2, 4, 2

mean:

$4 + 7 + 8 + 2 + 1 + 2 + 4 + 2 = 30$ Add the values.

$30 \div 8 = \boxed{}$ Divide the sum by the

$\boxed{}$.

The mean is $\boxed{}$.

median:

1, 2, 2, 2, 4, 4, 7, 8   Arrange the values in order.

$2 + 4 = 6$ Since there are two middle values, find the

$6 \div 2 = \boxed{}$ $\boxed{}$ of these two values.

The median is $\boxed{}$.

mode:

1, 2, 2, 2, 4, 4, 7, 8   The value $\boxed{}$ occurs three times.

The mode is $\boxed{}$.

range:

1, 2, 2, 2, 4, 4, 7, 8 $\boxed{}$ the least value from the

$8 - 1 = \boxed{}$ greatest value.

The range is $\boxed{}$.

Holt Mathematics

Example 2

The line plot shows the number of miles each of the 17 members of the cross-country team ran in a week. Which measure of central tendency best describes this data? Justify your answer.

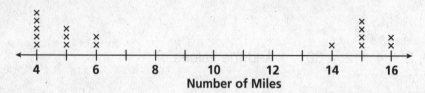

Number of Miles

mean:

$$\frac{4 + 4 + 4 + 4 + 4 + 5 + 5 + 5 + 6 + 6 + 14 + 15 + 15 + 15 + 15 + 16 + 16}{17}$$

$$= \frac{153}{17} = \boxed{}$$

The mean is [ ]. The mean [　　　　　　　] the data set because the data is clustered fairly evenly about two areas.

median:

4, 4, 4, 4, 4, 5, 5, 5, 6, 6, 14, 15, 15, 15, 15, 16, 16

The median is [ ]. The median [　　　　　　　　] the data

set because many values are not clustered around the data value 6.

Holt Mathematics

Example 3

The data shows Sara's scores for the last 5 math tests: 88, 90, 55, 94, and 89. Identify the outlier in the data set. Then determine how the outlier affects the mean, median, and mode of the data. Then tell which measure of central tendency best describes the data with the outlier.

The outlier is ☐ .

Without the Outlier

mean:

$\dfrac{88 + 89 + 90 + 94}{4} = \dfrac{361}{4} =$ ☐

median:

88, ☐ , ☐ , 94

$\dfrac{89 + 90}{2} =$ ☐

The median is ☐ .

mode:

There is no ☐ .

With the Outlier

mean:

$\dfrac{55 + 88 + 89 + 90 + 94}{5} = \dfrac{416}{5} =$ ☐

median:

55, 88, ☐ , 90, 94

The median is ☐ .

mode:

There is no ☐ .

Adding the outlier ▭ the mean by ▭ and the ▭ by 0.5.

The ▭ did not change.

Holt Mathematics

Check It Out!

1. Find the mean, median, mode, and range of the data set.

   6, 4, 3, 5, 2, 5, 1, 8

2. The line plot shows the number of dollars each of the 10 members of the cheerleading team raised in a week. Find the mean and median of the data. Which measure best describes this data? Justify your answer.

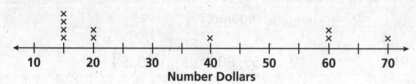

   Number Dollars

3. Identify the outlier in the data set. Then determine how the outlier affects the mean, median, and mode of the data.

   63, 58, 57, 61, 42

Holt Mathematics

LESSON 11-3 Box-and-Whisker Plots

Lesson Objectives

Display and analyze data in box-and-whisker plots

Vocabulary

lower quartile (p. 542) _____

upper quartile (p. 542) _____

_____

box-and-whisker plot (p. 543) _____

_____

_____

maximum (p. 543) _____

minimum (p. 543) _____

Additional Examples

Example 1

Find the lower and upper quartiles of each data set.

A. 15, 83, 75, 12, 19, 74, 21

[⬭] 21, [⬭] [ ] the values.

lower quartile: [ ]

upper quartile: [ ]

B. 75, 61, 88, 79, 79, 99, 63, 77

[⬭] [⬭] Order the values.

lower quartile: $\dfrac{[\quad]}{2}$ = [ ]

upper quartile: $\dfrac{[\quad]}{2}$ = [ ]

Holt Mathematics

Example 2

Use the given data to make a box-and-whisker plot.

21, 25, 15, 13, 17, 19, 19, 21

Step 1. Order the data and find the minimum, lower quartile, median, upper quartile, and maximum value.

```
┌──────────────────────────────────────────┐
│                                            │
└──────────────────────────────────────────┘
```

minimum: ▢

lower quartile: $\dfrac{\boxed{} + \boxed{}}{2}$ = ▢

median: $\dfrac{\boxed{} + \boxed{}}{2}$ = ▢

upper quartile: $\dfrac{\boxed{} + \boxed{}}{2}$ = ▢

maximum: ▢

Step 2. Draw a number line and plot a point above each value from Step 1.

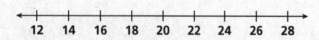

Step 3. Draw the box and whiskers.

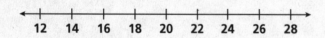

Holt Mathematics

Example 3

These box-and-whisker plots compare the ages of the first ten U.S. presidents with the ages of the last ten presidents (through George W. Bush) when they took office.

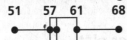

Age of First Ten Presidents at Inauguration

Age of Last Ten Presidents at Inauguration

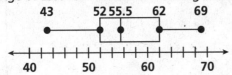

A. Compare the medians and ranges.

The median for the [ ] presidents is slightly greater. The range

for the [ ] presidents is greater.

B. Compare the ranges of the middle half of the data for each.

The range of the middle half of the data is greater for the [ ] presidents.

Holt Mathematics

Check It Out!

1. **Find the lower and upper quartiles for the data set.**
   45, 31, 59, 49, 49, 69, 33, 47

2. **Use the given data to make a box-and-whisker plot.**
   31, 23, 33, 35, 26, 24, 31, 29

3. **These box-and-whisker plots compare the points per quarter at Super Bowl XXXVII. Compare the medians and ranges.**

Quarter	1	2	3	4
Oakland	3	0	6	12
Tampa Bay	3	17	14	14

Oakland

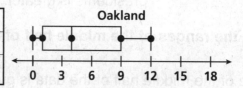

Tampa Bay

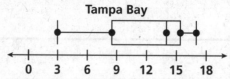

Scatter Plots

LESSON 11-4

Lesson Objectives

Create and interpret scatter plots

Vocabulary

scatter plot (p. 548) _____

_____

correlation (p. 549) _____

positive correlation (p. 549) _____

_____

negative correlation (p. 549) _____

_____

no correlation (p. 549) _____

_____

line of best fit (p. 549) _____

_____

Additional Examples

Example 1

Use the given data to make a scatter plot of the weight and height of each member of a basketball team.

Height (in.)	Weight (lb)
71	170
68	160
70	175
73	180
74	190

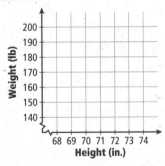

The points on the scatter plot are (_____), (_____),

(_____), (_____), and (_____).

Holt Mathematics

Example 2

Write *positive correlation, negative correlation,* or *no correlation* to describe the relationship. Explain.

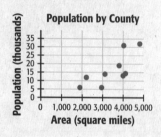

The graph shows that as area [_____], population

[_____]. So the graph shows [_____]

[_____] between the data sets.

Example 3

Use the data to predict how much a worker will earn in tips in 10 hours.

Hours	4	8	3	2	11
Tips ($)	12	20	7	7	26

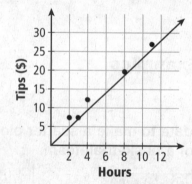

According to the graph a worker who works 10 hours should earn about

$[____].

Holt Mathematics

Check It Out!

1. Use the given data to make a scatter plot of the weight and height of each member of a soccer team.

Height (in)	Weight (lbs)
63	125
67	156
69	175
68	135
62	120

2. Write *positive correlation, negative correlation,* or *no correlation* to describe the relationship. Explain.

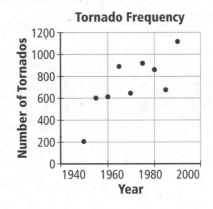

3. Use the data to predict how many circuit boards a worker will assemble in 10 hours.

Hours Worked	4	8	6	9	11
Circuit Board Assemblies	2	7	5	8	12

Holt Mathematics

Probability

LESSON 11-5

Lesson Objectives

Find the probability of an event by using the definition of probability

Vocabulary

experiment (p. 522) _____

_____

trial (p. 522) _____

_____

outcome (p. 522) _____

_____

sample space (p. 522) _____

_____

event (p. 522) _____

_____

probability (p. 522) _____

_____

Additional Examples

Example 1

Give the probability for the outcome.

A. The basketball team has a 70% chance of winning.

Outcome	Win	Lose
Probability	■	■

$P(\text{win}) = 70\% = $ [   ] .

$P(\text{lose}) = 1 - $ [   ] $= $ [   ] , or [   ] %.

Holt Mathematics

B.

Outcome	1	2	3
Probability	▦	▦	▦

$P(1) = \boxed{}$ Three of the eight sections of the spinner are labeled

1, so $\boxed{}$ is a reasonable estimate.

$P(2) = \boxed{}$ Three of the eight sections of the spinner are labeled

2, so $\boxed{}$ is a reasonable estimate.

$P(3) = \boxed{}$ Two of the eight sections of the spinner are labeled

3, so $\boxed{}$ is a reasonable estimate.

Check The probabilities of all the outcomes must add to $\boxed{}$.

$\boxed{} + \boxed{} + \boxed{} = \boxed{}$

Example 2

A quiz contains 5 true-false questions. Suppose you guess randomly on every question. The table below gives the probability of each score.

Score	0	1	2	3	4	5
Probability	0.031	0.156	0.313	0.313	0.156	0.031

A. What is the probability of guessing 3 or more correct?

The event "3 or more correct" consists of the outcomes $\boxed{}$, $\boxed{}$, and $\boxed{}$.

$P(3 \text{ or more correct}) = 0.\boxed{} + 0.\boxed{} + 0.\boxed{}$

$= \boxed{}$

B. What is the probability of guessing fewer than 2 correct?

The event "fewer than 2 correct" consists of the outcomes 0 and 1.

P(fewer than 2 correct) = [ ] + [ ] = [ ], or [ ]%.

Check It Out!

1. Give the probability for the outcome.
The polo team has a 50% chance of winning.

Outcome	Win	Lose
Probability		

2. A quiz contains 5 true-false questions. Suppose you guess randomly on every question. The table below gives the probability of each score. What is the probability of guessing fewer than 3 correct?

Score	0	1	2	3	4	5
Probability	0.031	0.156	0.313	0.313	0.156	0.031

Holt Mathematics

LESSON
11-6
Experimental Probability

Lesson Objectives

Estimate probability using experimental methods

Vocabulary

experimental probability (p. 560) _____

Additional Examples

Example 1

A marble is randomly drawn out of a bag and then replaced. The table shows the results after fifty draws.

Outcome	Green	Red	Yellow
Draw	12	15	23

A. Estimate the probability of drawing a red marble.

$$\text{probability} \approx \frac{\text{number of } \boxed{} \text{ marbles}}{\text{total number of draws}} = \frac{\boxed{}}{\boxed{}} = \boxed{}$$

The probability of drawing a red marble is about $\boxed{}$, or $\boxed{}$.

B. Estimate the probability of drawing a green marble.

$$\text{probability} \approx \frac{\text{number of } \boxed{} \text{ marbles}}{\text{total number of draws}} = \frac{\boxed{}}{\boxed{}} = \boxed{}$$

The probability of drawing a green marble is about $\boxed{}$, or $\boxed{}$.

Holt Mathematics

A marble is randomly drawn out of a bag and then replaced. The table shows the results after fifty draws.

Outcome	Green	Red	Yellow
Draw	12	15	23

C. Estimate the probability of drawing a yellow marble.

probability $\approx \dfrac{\text{number of } \boxed{} \text{ marbles}}{\text{total number of draws}} = \dfrac{\boxed{}}{\boxed{}} = \boxed{}$

The probability of drawing a yellow marble is about $\boxed{}$, or $\boxed{}$ %.

Example 2

Use the table to compare the probability that the Huskies will win their next game with the probability that the Knights will win their next game.

Team	Wins	Games
Huskies	79	138
Cougars	85	150
Knights	90	146

probability $\approx \dfrac{\text{number of wins}}{\text{number of games}}$

probability for a Huskies win $\approx \dfrac{\boxed{}}{\boxed{}} \approx \boxed{}$

probability for a Knights win $\approx \dfrac{\boxed{}}{\boxed{}} \approx \boxed{}$

The Knights are $\boxed{}$ likely to win their next game than the Huskies.

Check It Out!

1. A ticket is randomly drawn out of a bag and then replaced. The table shows the results after 100 draws. Estimate the probability of drawing a brown ticket.

Outcome	Purple	Orange	Brown
Draw	55	22	23

2. Use the table to compare the probability that the Huskies will win their next game with the probability that the Cougars will win their next game.

Team	Wins	Games
Huskies	79	138
Cougars	85	150
Knights	90	146

Holt Mathematics

LESSON
11-7

Theoretical Probability

Know it!
.Note

Lesson Objectives

Estimate probability using theoretical methods

Vocabulary

theoretical probability (p. 564) _____

_____

equally likely (p. 564) _____

fair (p. 564) _____

_____

mutually exclusive (p. 566) _____

_____

disjoint events (p. 566) _____

_____

Additional Examples

Example 1

An experiment consists of spinning this spinner once.
Find the probability of each event.

A. $P(4)$ The spinner is [   ], so all 5 outcomes are equally likely.

The probability of spinning a 4 is $P(4) =$ [   ] .

B. P(even number)   There are [   ] outcomes in the event of spinning an

even number: [   ] and [   ] .

P(even number) $= \dfrac{\text{number of possible } [\quad\quad] \text{ numbers}}{5} =$ [   ]

Holt Mathematics

Example 2

An experiment consists of rolling one fair number cube and flipping a coin. Find the probability of each event.

A. Show a sample space that has all outcomes equally likely.
The outcome of rolling a 5 and flipping heads can be written

as the ordered pair (5, H). There are ☐ possible outcomes.

B. *P*(tails)

There are ☐ outcomes in the event "flipping tails": (1, T), (2, T), (3, T),
(4, T), (5, T), and (6, T).

$P(\text{tails}) = $ ☐ $= $ ☐

Example 3

Stephany has 2 dimes and 3 nickels. How many pennies should be added so that the probability of drawing a nickel is $\frac{3}{7}$?

Adding pennies will ☐ the number of possible outcomes.

Let *x* equal the number of ☐ .

$\dfrac{3}{\boxed{}} = \dfrac{3}{7}$ Set up a proportion.

$3(5 + x) = 3(7)$ Find the cross products.

$15 + \boxed{} = \boxed{}$ Multiply.

$\boxed{} = \boxed{}$ Subtract ☐ from both sides.

$\dfrac{3x}{\boxed{}} = \dfrac{6}{\boxed{}}$ Divide both sides by ☐ .

$x = $ ☐

Stephany should add ☐ pennies so that the probability of drawing a
nickel is $\frac{3}{7}$.

Holt Mathematics

Check It Out!

1. An experiment consists of spinning this spinner once. Find the probability of the event.

$P(1)$

2. An experiment consists of flipping two coins. Find the probability of each event.

   $P(\text{both tails})$

3. Carl has 3 green buttons and 4 purple buttons. How many white buttons should be added so that the probability of drawing a purple button is $\frac{2}{9}$?

Holt Mathematics

LESSON 11-8
Independent and Dependent Events

Lesson Objectives

Find the probabilities of independent and dependent events

Vocabulary

compound event (p. 569) _____

_____

independent events (p. 569) _____

_____

dependent events (p. 569) _____

_____

Additional Examples

Example 1

Determine if the events are dependent or independent.

A. getting tails on a coin toss and rolling a 6 on a number cube

Tossing a coin does not affect rolling a number cube, so the two events are

_____ .

B. getting 2 red gumballs out of a gumball machine

After getting one red gumball out of a gumball machine, the chances for

getting the second red gumball have _____, so the two events

are _____ .

Holt Mathematics

Example 2

Three separate boxes each have one blue marble and one green marble. One marble is chosen from each box.

A. What is the probability of choosing a blue marble from each box?

The outcome of each choice does not affect the outcome of the other

choices, so the choices are ⬚.

In each box, P(blue) = ⬚.

P(blue, blue, blue) = ⬚ · ⬚ · ⬚ = ⬚ = ⬚   Multiply.

B. What is the probability of choosing a blue marble, then a green marble, and then a blue marble?

In each box, P(blue) = ⬚.

In each box, P(green) = ⬚.

P(blue, green, blue) = ⬚ · ⬚ · ⬚ = ⬚ = ⬚   Multiply.

C. What is the probability of choosing at least one blue marble?

Think: P(at least one blue) + P(not blue, not blue, not blue) = 1.

In each box, P(not blue) = ⬚.

P(not blue, not blue, not blue) = ⬚ · ⬚ · ⬚ = ⬚ = ⬚

Subtract from 1 to find the probability of choosing at least one blue marble.

1 − 0.125 = ⬚

Holt Mathematics

Example 3

The letters in the word *dependent* are placed in a box.

A. If two letters are chosen at random, without replacing the first letter, what is the probability that they will both be consonants?

$P(\text{first consonant}) = \boxed{} = \boxed{}$

If the first letter chosen was a consonant, now there would be 5 consonants and a total of 8 letters left in the box. Find the probability that the second letter chosen is a consonant.

$P(\text{second consonant}) = \boxed{}$

$\boxed{} \cdot \boxed{} = \boxed{}$ Multiply.

The probability of choosing two letters that are both consonants is $\boxed{}$.

B. If two letters are chosen at random, without replacing the first letter, what is the probability that they will both be consonants or both be vowels?

The probability of two consonants was calculated in Additional Example 3A. Now find the probability of getting two vowels.

$P(\text{vowel}) = \boxed{} = \boxed{}$ Find the probability that the first letter chosen is a vowel.

If the first letter chosen is a vowel, there are now only $\boxed{}$ vowels and $\boxed{}$ total letters left.

$P(\text{vowel}) = \boxed{} = \boxed{}$ Find the probability that the second letter chosen is a vowel.

$\frac{1}{3} \cdot \frac{1}{4} = \boxed{}$ Multiply.

The events of both letters being consonants or both being vowels are mutually exclusive, so you can add their probabilities.

$\frac{5}{12} + \boxed{} = \boxed{} = \boxed{}$ $P(\text{consonants}) + P(\text{vowels})$

The probability of both letters being consonants or both being vowels is $\boxed{}$.

Holt Mathematics

Check It Out!

1. Determine if the events are dependent or independent.

   a computer randomly generating two of the same numbers in a row

2. Two boxes each contain 4 marbles: red, blue, green, and black. One marble is chosen from each box.

   What is the probability of choosing a blue marble from each box?

3. The letters in the phrase *I Love Math* are placed in a box.

   If two letters are chosen at random, without replacing the first letter, what is the probability that they will both be consonants or both be vowels?

Holt Mathematics

CHAPTER 11

Chapter Review

11-1 Line Plots and Stem-and-Leaf Plots

The list shows the time in minutes that students spend on the Internet.

65, 38, 44, 27, 65, 48, 52, 15, 44, 35

1. Make a line plot of the data.

2. Make a stem-and-leaf plot of the table.

11-2 Mean, Median, Mode, and Range

The list shows the ages of men on a tennis team.

23, 40, 42, 34, 31, 36, 49, 58, 25, 36, 28

3. Find the mean, median, and mode, and range of the data. Round your answers to the nearest tenth of a year.

4. Which measure of central tendency best represents the data? Explain.

11-3 Box-and-Whisker Plots

Find the lower and upper quartiles for the data set.

5. 29, 65, 89, 57, 85, 37, 52, 68, 45

Use the given data to make a box-and-whisker plot.

6. 8, 4, 5, 7, 9, 10, 6, 5, 8, 11, 12, 8, 9, 5, 7, 8, 7, 6, 5, 5, 4

Holt Mathematics

11-4 Scatter Plots

7. The table shows the calories and fat in selected meals at a restaurant. Use the data to make a scatter plot.

Calories	Fat
285	6
400	7
375	9
550	12
600	16
950	19
1,200	24

8. Does the scatter plot indicate a positive, a negative, or no correlation?

11-5 Probability

Use the table to find the probability of each event.

Outcome	A	B	C	D
Probability	0.6	0.05	0.25	0.1

9. C occurring

10. D not occurring

11. A or C occurring

12. B, C, or D occurring

13. There are 4 students in a race. Horace has a 40% chance of winning. Paul, Lance, and Jameson all have the same chance of winning. Create a table of probabilities for the sample space.

Holt Mathematics

11-6 Experimental Probability

An experiment consists of spinning a spinner with the colors red, green, blue, and yellow. The experiment is repeated 200 times with the following results.

Outcome	red	green	blue	yellow
Spins	59	22	106	13

14. Estimate the probability of each outcome. Create a table of probability for the sample space.

15. Find P(blue or green).

16. Find P(not yellow).

17. Find P(red, blue, or yellow).

18. Find P(not red).

11-7 Theoretical Probability

An experiment consists of rolling two fair number cubes. Find the probability of each event.

19. P(product shown = 12)

20. P(two prime numbers)

11-8 Independent and Dependent Events

21. An experiment consists of tossing three fair coins, two quarters and a dime. Determine whether the outcome of the events is dependent or independent. Find the probability of heads on both quarters and tails on the dime.

22. A jar contains 10 blue marbles and 6 purple marbles. If three marbles are chosen at random, what is the probability that the first two will be purple and the next will be blue?

Holt Mathematics

Answer these questions to summarize the important concepts from Chapter 7 in your own words.

1. Explain how to find the mean, median, mode, and range of the data set.

   5, 8, 10, 12, 6, 5, 3

2. Explain the difference between positive and negative correlation.

3. An experiment consists of tossing three coins. Explain how to find the probability of each coin landing on heads.

For more review of Chapter 11:

- Complete the Chapter 11 Study Guide: Review on pages 578–580 of your textbook.

- Complete the Ready to Go On quizzes on pages 554 and 574 of your textbook.

Holt Mathematics

LESSON
12-1

Polynomials

Lesson Objectives

Classify polynomials by degree and by the number of terms

Vocabulary

polynomial (p. 590) _____

_____

binomial (p. 590) _____

_____

trinomial (p. 590) _____

_____

degree of a polynomial (p. 591) _____

_____

Additional Examples

Example 1

Determine whether each expression is a monomial.

A. $\sqrt{2} \cdot x^3y^4$

[   ]

3 and 4 are [   ] numbers.

B. $3x^3\sqrt{y}$

[   ]

y does not have an [   ] that is a whole number.

Holt Mathematics

Example 2

Classify each expression as a monomial, a binomial, a trinomial, or not a polynomial. Explain your answer.

A. xy^2

Polynomial with ☐ term.

B. $2x^2 - 4y^{-2}$

A variable with a ☐ exponent.

C. $3x^5 + 2.2x^2 - 4$

Polynomial with ☐ terms.

D. $a^2 + b^2$

Polynomial with ☐ terms.

Example 3

Find the degree of each polynomial.

A. $x + 4$

x $+$ 4

Degree ☐   Degree ☐

The degree of $x + 4$ is ☐.

B. $5x - 2x^2 + 6$

$5x$ $-$ $2x^2$ $+$ 6

Degree ☐   Degree ☐   Degree ☐

The degree of $5x - 2x^2 + 6$ is ☐.

Holt Mathematics

Example 4

The height in feet after t seconds of a rocket launched straight up into the air from a 40-foot platform at velocity v is given by the polynomial $-16t^2 + vt + 40$. Find the height after 10 seconds of a rocket launched at a velocity of 275 ft/s.

$-16t^2 + vt + 40$ Write the polynomial expression for height.

$-16(\boxed{})^2 + \boxed{} (\boxed{}) + 40$ Substitute 10 for t and 275 for v.

$\boxed{} + \boxed{} + 40$ Simplify.

$\boxed{}$

The rocket is $\boxed{}$ ft high 10 seconds after launching.

Check It Out!

1. Determine whether the expression is a monomial.

   $2w \cdot p^3 y^8$

2. Classify the expression as a monomial, a binomial, a trinomial, or not a polynomial.

   $4x^2 + 7z^4$

3. Find the degree of the polynomial.

   $x + 4x^4 + 2y$

4. The height in feet after t seconds of a rocket launched straight up into the air from a 20-foot platform at velocity v is given by the polynomial $-16t^2 + vt + 20$. Find the height after 15 seconds of the rocket launched at a velocity of 250 ft/s.

Holt Mathematics

Simplifying Polynomials

LESSON 12-2

Lesson Objectives

Simplify polynomials

Additional Examples

Example 1

Identify the like terms in each polynomial.

A. $5x^3 + y^2 + 2 - 6y^2 + 4x^3$

$5x^3 + y^2 + 2 - 6y^2 + 4x^3$ Identify like terms.

Like terms: $5x^3$ and [ ], y^2 and [ ]

B. $3a^3b^2 + 3a^2b^3 + 2a^3b^2 - a^3b^2$

$3a^3b^2 + 3a^2b^3 + 2a^3b^2 - a^3b^2$ Identify [ ] terms.

Like terms: [ ], [ ], and [ ]

C. $7p^3q^2 + 7p^2q^3 + 7pq^2$

$7p^3q^2 + 7p^2q^3 + 7pq^2$ Identify [ ].

There are [ ] like terms.

Example 2

Simplify.

A. $4x^2 + 2x^2 + 7 - 6x + 9$

$4x^2 + 2x^2 - 6x + 7 + 9$ Arrange in descending order.

$4x^2 + 2x^2 - 6x + 7 + 9$ Identify like terms.

[ ]   Combine coefficients:

                             $4 + 2 = 6$ and $7 + 9 = 16$

Holt Mathematics

B. $3n^5m^4 - 6n^3m + n^5m^4 - 8n^3m$

$3n^5m^4 + n^5m^4 - 6n^3m - 8n^3m$ Arrange in descending order.

$3n^5m^4 + n^5m^4 - 6n^3m - 8n^3m$ Identify like terms.

Combine coefficients:

$3 + 1 = 4$ and $-6 - 8 = -14$

Example 3

Simplify.

A. $3(x^3 + 5x^2)$

$3(x^3 + 5x^2)$ Distributive Property

$3 \cdot x^3 + 3 \cdot 5x^2$

B. $-4(3m^3n + 7m^2n) + m^2n$

$-4(3m^3n + 7m^2n) + m^2n$ Distributive Property

$-4 \cdot 3m^3n - 4 \cdot 7m^2n + m^2n$

$-12m^3n - 28m^2n + m^2n$

    Combine like terms.

Example 4

The surface area of a right cylinder can be found by using the expression $2\pi(r^2 + rh)$, where *r* is the radius and *h* is the height. Use the Distributive Property to write an equivalent expression.

$2\pi(r^2 + rh) = $

Holt Mathematics

Check It Out!

1. Identify the like terms in the polynomial.

$4y^4 + y^2 + 2 - 8y^2 + 2y^4$

2. Simplify.

$2x^3 + 5x^3 + 6 - 4x + 9$

3. Simplify.

$-2(6m^3p + 8m^2p) + m^2p$

4. Use the Distributive Property to write an equivalent expression
$3a(b^2 + c)$.

Holt Mathematics

LESSON 12-3 **Adding Polynomials**

Lesson Objectives

Add polynomials

Additional Examples

Example 1

Add.

A. $(5x^3 + x^2 + 2) + (4x^3 + 6x^2)$

$5x^3 + x^2 + 2 + 4x^3 + 6x^2$ Associative Property

[ ] $x^3 + $ [ ] $x^2 + 2$ Combine [ ] terms.

B. $(6x^3 + 8y^2 + 5xy) + (4xy - 2y^2)$

$6x^3 + 8y^2 + 5xy + 4xy - 2y^2$ Associative Property

[ ]   Combine [ ] terms.

C. $(3x^2y - 5x) + (4x + 7) + 6x^2y$

$3x^2y - 5x + 4x + 7 + 6x^2y$ Associative Property

[ ] $x^2y - $ [ ] $ + 7$ Combine [ ] terms.

Example 2

Add.

A. $(4x^2 + 2x + 11) + (2x^2 + 6x + 9)$

$4x^2 + 2x + 11$

$\underline{+ \; 2x^2 + 6x + 9}$ Place like terms in columns.

[ ]   Combine [ ] terms.

B. $(3mn^2 - 6m + 6n) + (5mn^2 + 2m - n)$

$3mn^2 - 6m + 6n$

$\underline{+ \; 5mn^2 + 2m - n}$ Place like [ ] in columns.

[ ]   Combine [ ] terms.

Holt Mathematics

C. $(-x^2y^2 + 5x^2) + (-2y^2 + 2) + (x^2 + 8)$

$$-x^2y^2 + 5x^2$$

$$-2y^2 + 2$$

$$+ \quad\quad x^2 \quad\quad + 8$$

Place like [   ] in columns.

Combine [   ] terms.

Example 3

Rachel wants to frame two photographs. The first photograph has dimensions *b* inches and *h* inches, and each dimension of the other photograph is twice the corresponding dimensions of the first. She needs enough wood for the frames to cover both perimeters, and the width of the wood is $1\frac{1}{2}$ inches. Find an expression for the length of wood she needs to frame both photographs.

The amount of wood Rachel needs equals the perimeter of both frames. Draw a diagram to help you determine the dimensions of the frame.

$1\frac{1}{2}$ in. — *h* in. — *b* in.

$1\frac{1}{2}$ in. — 2*h* in. — 2*b* in.

perimeter of first photograph = 2([   ] + [   ]) + 2([   ] + [   ])

$$= [\quad] + 6 + 2h + [\quad]$$

$$= 2b + 2h + [\quad]$$

perimeter of second photograph = 2([   ] + [   ]) + 2([   ] + [   ])

$$= 4b + [\quad] + [\quad] + 6$$

$$= 4b + 4h + [\quad]$$

Holt Mathematics

perimeter of both photographs = $2b + 2h + 12 + 4b + 4h + 12$

$$= \boxed{} + \boxed{} + \boxed{}$$

Rachel will need ⬚ inches of wood to frame both photographs.

Check It Out!

1. Add.

$(3y^4 + y^2 + 6) + (5y^4 + 2y^2)$

2. Add.

$(4mn^2 + 6m + 2n) + (2mn^2 - 2m - 2n)$

3. Michael wants to frame two photographs. The first photograph had dimensions *b* inches and *h* inches, and each dimension of the other photograph is three times the corresponding dimension of the first. He needs enough wood for the frames to cover both perimeters and the width of the wood is 2 inches. Find an expression for the length of wood he will need to frame both photographs.

California Standards Prev. of Algebra 1, ←10.0, ←7AF1.3

Subtracting Polynomials

LESSON 12-4

Lesson Objectives

Subtract polynomials

Additional Examples

Example 1

Find the opposite of each polynomial.

A. $8x^3y^4z^2$

$-(8x^3y^4z^2)$

[   ]   The opposite of a is [   ].

B. $-3x^4 + 8x^2$

$-(-3x^4 + 8x^2)$

[   ]   Distributive Property.

C. $9a^6b^4 + a^4b^2 - 1$

$-(9a^6b^4 + a^4b^2 - 1)$

[   ]   Distributive Property.

Example 2

Subtract.

A. $(5x^2 + 2x - 3) - (3x^2 + 8x - 4)$

$= (5x^2 + 2x - 3)\ [\ ]\ (\ [\ ]\ 3x^2\ [\ ]\ 8x\ [\ ]\ 4)$ Add the opposite.

$= 5x^2 + 2x - 3 - 3x^2 - 8x + 4$ [   ] Property.

$= $ [   ]   Combine like terms.

B. $(b^2 + 4b - 1) - (7b^2 - b - 1)$

$= (b^2 + 4b - 1)\ [\ ]\ (\ [\ ]\ 7b^2\ [\ ]\ b\ [\ ]\ 1)$ Add the opposite.

$= b^2 + 4b - 1 - 7b^2 + b + 1$ [   ] Property.

$= $ [   ]   Combine like terms.

Holt Mathematics

Example 3

Subtract.

A. $(2n^2 - 4n + 9) - (6n^2 - 7n + 5)$

$(2n^2 - 4n + 9)2n^2 - 4n + 9$

$\underline{-\ (6n^2 - 7n + 5)} \rightarrow \underline{+\ -6n^2 + 7n - 5}$

Add the opposite.

B. $(10x^2 + 2x - 7) - (x^2 + 5x + 1)$

$(10x^2 + 2x - 7)10x^2 + 2x - 7$

$\underline{-\ (x^2 + 5x + 1)} \rightarrow \underline{+\ -x^2 - 5x - 1}$

Add the opposite.

C. $(6a^4 - 3a^2 - 8) - (-2a^4 + 7)$

$(6a^4 - 3a^2 - 8)6a^4 - 3a^2 - 8$

$\underline{-\ (-2a^4 + 7)} \rightarrow \underline{+\ 2a^4 - 7}$

Example 4

Suppose the cost in dollars of producing x bookcases is given by the polynomial $250 + 128x$, and the revenue generated from sales is given by the polynomial $216x - 75$. Find a polynomial expression for the profit from producing and selling x bookcases, and evaluate the expression for $x = 95$.

$216x - 75 - (250 + 128x)$ \qquad revenue $-$ cost

$216x - 75 + (\boxed{} - \boxed{})$ \quad Add the opposite.

$216x - 75 - 250 - 128x$ \qquad Associative Property

$\boxed{}\ x - \boxed{}$ \qquad Combine like terms.

The profit is given by the polynomial $\boxed{}$.

For $x = 95$,

$88(\boxed{}) - 325 = \boxed{}$ \qquad The profit is $\$\boxed{}$.

Holt Mathematics

Check It Out!

1. Find the opposite of the polynomial.

   $-4a^2 + 4a^4$

2. Subtract.

   $(c^3 + 2c^2 + 3) - (4c^3 - c^2 - 1)$

3. Subtract.

   $(4r^3 + 4r + 6) - (6r^3 + 3r + 3)$

4. Suppose the cost in dollars of producing x baseball bats is given by the polynomial $6 + 12x$, and the revenue generated from sales is given by the polynomial $35x - 5$. Find a polynomial expression for the profit from producing and selling x baseball bats, and evaluate the expression for $x = 50$.

Holt Mathematics

California Standards Prev. of Algebra 1, ←10.0, 7AF1.2,←7AF1.3, 7AF2.2

LESSON 12-5
Multiplying Polynomials by Monomials

Lesson Objectives

Multiply polynomials by monomials

Additional Examples

Example 1

Multiply.

$(2x^3y^2)(6x^5y^3)$

$(2x^3y^2)(6x^5y^3)$

[　　　　　] [　　　　] coefficients and [　　]

exponents that have the same [　　　].

Example 2

Multiply.

$3m(5m^2 + 2m)$

$3m(5m^2 + 2m)$ Multiply each term in parentheses by [　　].

[　　　　　　]

Example 3

The length of a picture in a frame is 8 in. less than three times its width. Find the length and width if the area is 60 in².

1. **Understand the Problem**

   If the width of the frame is w and the length is $3w - 8$, then the area is

   [　　　　　　] or length times width. The answer will be a value of

   w that makes the area of the frame equal to 60 in².

2. **Make a Plan**

   You can make a table of values for the polynomial to try to find the value of

   a w. Use the [　　　　　　　　] Property to write the expression

   $w(3w - 8)$ another way. Use substitution to complete the table.

Holt Mathematics

3. Solve

$$w(3w - 8) = \boxed{}\, w^2 - \boxed{}\, w \qquad \boxed{} \text{ Property}$$

w	3	4	5	6
$3w^2 - 8w$				

The width should be [ ] in. and the length should be [ ] in.

4. Look Back

If the width is [ ] inches and the length is [ ] times that minus 8, or 10

inches, then the area would be $6 \cdot 10 = \boxed{}$ in². The answer is reasonable.

Check It Out!

1. Multiply.

$$(5r^4s^3)(3r^3s^2)$$

2. Multiply.

$$-3a^3b^2(4ab^3 + 4a^2)$$

3. The height of a triangle is twice its base. Find the base and the height if the area is 144 in².

Holt Mathematics

Multiplying Binomials

LESSON **12-6**

Lesson Objectives

Multiply binomials

Vocabulary

FOIL (p. 618) _____

Additional Examples

Example 1

Multiply.

A. $(n - 2)(m - 8)$

$(n - 2)(m - 8)$　　FOIL

B. $(x + 3)(x + z)$

$(x + 3)(x + z)$　　FOIL

Example 2

An 8 in. by 10 in. photo has a wooden frame that extends x in. beyond each side. Represent the area of the frame in terms of x.

$$\text{Area of Frame} = \text{Total Area} - \text{Area of Photo}$$

$$= (8 + 2x)(10 + 2x) - (8)(10)$$

$$= \boxed{} + \boxed{}x + \boxed{}x + \boxed{}x^2 - \boxed{}$$

$$= \boxed{}x + \boxed{}x^2$$

The frame area is $\boxed{}x + \boxed{}x^2$ in.^{2}.

Holt Mathematics

Example 3

Multiply.

A. $(x + 6)^2$

$(x + 6)(x + 6)$

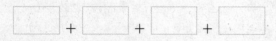

B. $(n - m)^2$

$(n - m)(n - m)$

Check It Out!

1. Multiply.

$(r - 4)(s - 6)$

2. Find the area of the border around a computer monitor of width x centimeters around a 50 cm by 80 cm screen. Represent the area of the border in terms of x.

3. Multiply.

$(r - 3)^2$

Holt Mathematics

Chapter Review

12-1 Polynomials

Classify each expression as a monomial, a binomial, a trinomial, or not a polynomial. If it is a polynomial, give its degree.

1. $-7x^4$

2. $-\dfrac{5}{x} + 2$

3. $5x^{0.3} + 4x$

4. $\dfrac{8}{9}x - \dfrac{4}{5}x^2$

5. $3z^5 + 5z^2 - 6z$ **6.** -6

7. $\dfrac{2y^3}{6x^2}$

8. $8y - 6$

9. The volume of a box with length x, width $x + 3$, and height $2x - 1$ is given by the trinomial $2x^3 + 5x^2 - 3x$. What is the volume of the box if the length is 3 inches?

12-2 Simplifying Polynomials

Simplify.

10. $4r^2 - 8r + 7r^2 + 6r - 5$

11. $-7x^2y + 8xy - 9xy^2 - 6x^2y + 3xy^2$

12. $3(x^2 - 4x + 3) - 7x + 1$

13. $4yz + y^3z^2 + 2(3y^3z^2 - 5yz)$

12-3 Adding Polynomials

Add.

14. $(4a^2b - 3ab + 2) + (8ab - 3a^2b)$

15. $(7f + 2) + (4f^2 - 3f + 6)$

16. $(3g^3 + 7g - 5g^5) + (10g^5 + 8g^3 - 3g)$ **17.** $(6p^2 + 2p - 9) + (3p^2 - 5p + 4)$

18. The cost of baking n cakes is given by the polynomial $2.5n^2 + n + 2$. The cost of packaging n cakes is $0.1n^2 + 0.3n + 1.5$. Write and simplify an expression for the total cost of baking and packaging n cakes.

Holt Mathematics

12-4 Subtracting Polynomials

Subtract.

19. $(12b^2 + 5b + 3) - (3b^2 - 4b - 7)$

20. $(9x^2y^2 - 4xy^2 + 8x^2y - xy) - (2x^2y - 5x^2y^2 + 2xy)$

21. $(8r^2s^2 + 6rs - 6r + 7) - (3r^2s^2 + 2r - 9s - 5)$

22. The area of the rectangle is $3b^2 - 2b + 5$ cm². The area of the square is $2b^2 - 3b + 1$ cm². What is the area of the shaded region?

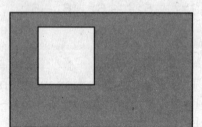

12-5 Multiplying Polynomials and Monomials

Multiply.

23. $(5p^3q^2)(3pq^4)$

24. $-6a^4(2a^2 + 3a)$

25. $b^5(b^3c^2 + c - b^2)$

26. $(6mn)(8m^3n^2 + 3m^2n^3 - 2mn^4)$

27. A rectangle has a base length of $2xy^2$ and a height of $3x^2 - xy + 5$. Write and simplify an expression for the area of the rectangle. Then find the area of the rectangle if $x = 1$ and $y = 2$.

12-6 Multiplying Binomials

Multiply.

28. $(k - 5)(k - 8)$

29. $(c - 10)(c + 10)$

30. $(3v - 6)^2$

31. $(4p + 7)(2p - 9)$

32. $(5a + b)(a + 7b)$

33. $(4s + 11t)^2$

34. A painting measures 16 in. by 20 in. There is a frame of x in. around the painting. Find the total area of the frame and the painting.

Holt Mathematics

CHAPTER 12 **Big Ideas**

Answer these questions to summarize the important concepts from Chapter 14 in your own words.

1. Explain why $2\sqrt{x}$ is not a monomial.

2. Explain how to simplify the polynomial.
$a^3 + 4a^5 - 3a^2 + 2 - 6a^2 + 8a^5$

3. Explain how to subtract the polynomials horizontally.
$(b^3 - 7 + b^2) - (4b + 3 - 3b^3)$

4. Explain how to multiply the polynomial by the monomial.
$0.5y^2(yz^5 - 8xy^3)$

5. Explain how to multiply the binomials using the FOIL method.
$(7c - 3)(c + 9)$

For more review of Chapter 12:

- Complete the Chapter 12 Study Guide and Review on pages 626–628 of your textbook.

- Complete the Ready to Go On quizzes on pages 600 and 622 of your textbook.

Holt Mathematics